Edinburgh

EDINBURGH

A Travellers' Companion

SELECTED AND INTRODUCED BY

David Daiches

Constable London

First published in Great Britain 1986
by Constable and Company Limited
10 Orange Street London WC2H 7EG
Copyright © 1986 by David Daiches
Set in Monophoto Baskerville 11pt
by Servis Filmsetting Ltd, Manchester
Printed in Great Britain by
St Edmundsbury Press
Bury St Edmunds, Suffolk

British Library CIP data
Edinburgh: a traveller's companion. – (The
Traveller's companion series)
1. Edinburgh (Lothian) – Social life and customs
I. Daiches, David   II. Series
941.3′4   DA890.E2

ISBN 0 09 465010 1 (hardback)
ISBN 0 09 465950 8 (paperback)

Contents

Illustrations

Acknowledgements

I should like to thank the following for permission to use extracts from their books or editions: Newnes Books, a division of the Hamlyn Publishing Group Ltd, for Eric Linklater's *Edinburgh*; Mainstream Publishing for *A Scottish Journey* by Edwin Muir; Oxford University Press for the excerpt from Defoe's letter to Robert Harley on 24 October 1706, from *The Letters of Daniel Defoe* (pp. 133–135) edited by George Harris Healey; and to John Murray for *Memoirs of a Highland Lady* by Elizabeth Grant, revised and edited by Angus Davidson.

I am also grateful to Mrs Armstrong, Head of the Reference and Information Services at the Central Library, Edinburgh, for her help with the illustrations; and my warmest thanks are due to Rosanna Neville and Margaret Jardine for heroic work at the typewriter.

D.D.
1985

Introduction

Edinburgh is a city whose history is written on its face. The turbulence of its early centuries is even today evoked by the appearance of the 'Royal Mile' running from the Castle to the Abbey and Palace of Holyrood. This, and its immediate environs, represent the core of the Old Town, and centuries of 'progress' have not significantly changed its atmosphere. Executions, murders, riots, processions, celebrations – the history of the Old Town is packed with these, as the following pages will show. Old names like Lawnmarket, Grassmarket, Cowgate, Canongate, survive to remind us of Edinburgh's past, while to the north the elegant street patterns and classical buildings suggest a quieter and more rational world, that of the New Town, evoking the ideals of order and 'improvement' of the Edinburgh literati of the late eighteenth century. If you walk from the High Street down the Mound to Princes Street and then to the streets running parallel to Princes Street to the north, you are walking from the Middle Ages to the Age of Enlightenment; if you go south across the Meadows to the Marchmont and Warrender area, the sombre rows of solidly built flats show that you have emerged into the respectabilities of the Victorian middle class. There are all kinds of social, architectural and topographical distinctions in between these, and one of the pleasures of walking in Edinburgh is discovering them and reading the social, political, and even intellectual history of the city in its streets and buildings.

Edinburgh's history over many centuries was shadowed by the continual struggle of English kings to dominate Scotland. Then the Reformation brought both religious and political feuding, with Covenanters against Royalist Episcopalians, and the public execution in the city of the Marquis of Montrose on the Royalist side and of two successive Earls of Argyll on the covenanting side shocking the populace into an awareness of the price of such conflicts while at the same time providing them with memorable exhibitions.

The fierce debates that took place in the Scottish Parliament in Edinburgh in the four years preceding the Union of 1707 were reflected in popular unrest and street rioting. The Edinburgh mob in the early eighteenth century was a force to be reckoned with, as the Porteous Riots of 1736 so clearly demonstrate, but as the century proceeded the ideals of the Scottish Enlightenment prevailed more and more, and Edinburgh became increasingly respectable. By Victorian times it was such a respectable city, at least on the surface, that it provoked rebellion on the part of young bohemians like Robert Louis Stevenson.

Edinburgh was never, however, a homogeneous city. Theological passion and a love of dancing, like love of theatrical shows and a bitter religious disapproval of the theatre, could co-exist in the seventeenth and eighteenth centuries; and even in its most Calvinist moods the city rarely missed an occasion for celebration. Edinburgh and its inhabitants could be both drab and colourful, self-controlled and passionate, dull and exciting. Today, with the Edinburgh International Festival annually giving the old gray city a lively continental air, these contradictions are as visible as ever.

Long before Edinburgh emerged into history, volcanic activity had formed the rocks and hills over which later slow glacier movement carved the shapes which were to determine the pattern of the medieval city. The rock on which a fortress was built by the ancient British inhabitants – called in British Celtic 'Dineiden', 'fortress of the hill slope', 'Dun-Eideann' in Gaelic – lies at the western edge of a ridge on which the original city was constructed. The present Edinburgh Castle is the descendant of that original fortress, which was many times rebuilt throughout the centuries, and the name 'Edinburgh' represents the replacement of the Celtic 'Din' by the Old English equivalent 'Burgh' as a result of the conquest of a considerable part of southern Scotland by Northumbrians in the seventh century. But the Gaelic-speaking MacAlpin line of kings pushed east and south from their Argyllshire base and by the tenth century had made Dunedin, as they called it (though the Anglian form of

Edinburgh remained, and eventually took over), a part of
Scotland.

Under the shelter of the protective fortress to the west,
merchants and others settled, and by 1329, when King Robert I
granted to the burgh of Edinburgh its earliest surviving charter,
it was clearly a centre of some importance, with the Abbey of
Holyrood, founded by David I in 1128, lying at the eastern end
of the ridge running from the Castle: first the Castle, then the
Lawnmarket and the High Street, then (entering now the
separate burgh of Canongate) eastward along the Canongate
(Canons' Way or Road) to Holyrood. Along this line the city of
Edinburgh grew up, crowded, noisy and smelly. Significant
expansion to the north and south of the ridge was made difficult
by natural features. To the north were marshy ground and the
Craig Burn which was dammed and made into the Nor' Loch for
defensive purposes in the mid-fifteenth century; and although
the Grassmarket and the Cowgate developed in the fifteenth
century to the south below the Castle and the eastward ridge, the
lie of the land was not conducive to further southward expansion
on any scale. Essentially, the shape of medieval Edinburgh was
that of a herring-bone, with little 'wynds' and 'closes' going off at
right angles from the main spine, packed with wood-framed
houses.

This shape remained until the second part of the eighteenth
century. In general, it could be said that before the mid-
eighteenth century the city expanded upward rather than
sideways, with tall buildings ('lands') that were the astonishment of visitors accommodating numbers of families in what
might almost be called vertical streets. We first see it as a city of
merchants and craftsmen, but also increasingly as a royal city.
Malcolm III made the Castle a principal if intermittent royal
residence in the eleventh century, and in 1124 David I made it a
permanent royal residence. The Palace of Holyroodhouse was
founded by James IV in 1498, beside the Abbey. Though the
concept of a capital city was slow to develop, the Stewart kings
gradually came to accept Edinburgh as the chief city of their
kingdom and by the sixteenth century it was generally regarded
as the capital.

It was in the eighteenth century that the city began to expand on any real scale, first to the south, between the High Street and the Burgh Loch (which was partially drained in the late sixteenth century, and fully drained, to become the Meadows, in the eighteenth); then to the north after the draining of the Nor' Loch and the bridging of the valley. But the city of which we get the first descriptions is the medieval city, the crowded town on the ridge, with the Nor' Loch to the north, the Grassmarket and the Cowgate to the south, and its centre in the broad High Street by the High Kirk of St Giles, the old Tolbooth, and the Mercat Cross. The Mercat Cross stood at the south side of the High Street, east of St Giles's, from the fourteenth century until 1756; in 1885 William Ewart Gladstone was responsible for the erection of a restored Cross on the old site.

Attempts by successive English kings to subdue Scotland were finally defeated by Scotland's victory over England at the battle of Bannockburn in 1314, but this did not mean that English armies were no longer a threat to Edinburgh. After the disastrous defeat of the Scottish army at Flodden in 1513, when James IV and the flower of his nobility were killed, Edinburgh anticipated an attack by the English army and built the famous Flodden wall as a defence. (The attack did not in fact materialize.) This wall, which was not finished until 1560, defined the Ancient Royalty or official limits of the burgh of Edinburgh for more than two centuries.

The 1540s were a particularly dangerous time for Edinburgh. On the death of James V in 1542, which left his infant daughter, Mary, as Queen of Scots, pro-French and pro-English factions confronted each other. Henry VIII tried to dissuade the Scots from looking to her old ally France and arranging a French marriage for Mary, by trying to arrange a marriage between Mary and his son Edward; and when the pro-French faction blocked this, he sent the Earl of Hertford to Scotland with an army designed to coerce the Scots into agreeing to his scheme: this was known as the 'rough wooing'. The Earl of Hertford's army landed at Leith and proceeded to burn much of Edinburgh, including the abbey and palace of Holyrood: a contemporary drawing shows the burnt roofs of houses flanking the

High Street, but also indicates that behind the wooden fronts were walls of stone, which survived. Edinburgh was attacked again by the Duke of Somerset's army in 1547, when much damage was inflicted. The terrorizing of Edinburgh by English troops only stopped after the arrival of a French army in 1548 and the defeat of English forces in France in 1550.

The Scottish Parliament of 1560 formally proclaimed Protestantism the religion of the country and ushered in a period of civil strife marked by conflict between the pro-French and pro-Mary Catholic faction and their Protestant opponents. In 1561 Mary returned from France, where she had spent the preceding thirteen years, landing at Leith before making a ceremonial entry into Edinburgh. Within six years her enemies had prevailed and she was forced to abdicate in favour of her infant son. When he was thirteen years old, in 1579, James VI made a ceremonial entry into Edinburgh. As he grew older, and defined and asserted his policies, it became clear that his favouring of episcopacy as the proper form of church government ('No Bishop, No King') would lead to clashes with Scottish Presbyterians, and such clashes became a feature of Scottish history and of Edinburgh life in the reign of King James and of his son Charles I.

James was a literate, indeed a pedantic, king, and he encouraged the Town Council of Edinburgh to build a College for the town, granting a royal charter for that purpose in 1582. In 1617, pleased with its progress, he ordered that the Town's College, as it was generally called, should be known in future by the name of King James's College. This is now the University of Edinburgh.

When James VI inherited the throne of England in 1603 and went south to become James I of England (while retaining his title of James VI of Scotland), Edinburgh ceased to be a city housing a royal court. James boasted that after 1603 he governed Scotland by his pen, but although political power now lay in the south, Scotland, with its fierce religious passions and the commitment of much of its Lowland population to Presbyterianism and Calvinism, played a crucial part in the civil wars of the seventeenth century, when Edinburgh was deeply involved in the protests against Charles I's attempts to impose Anglican forms on Scottish worship, and in the shifting political attitudes of Presbyterians. Charles I was crowned King of Scotland (not, as was traditional, King of Scots) in the Abbey Church of Holyrood in 1633, and in the same year made Edinburgh into an episcopal see, so that the High Kirk of St Giles now became St Giles's Cathedral, which it remained until the abolition of episcopacy in the Church of Scotland in 1639. (It was re-established as a cathedral at the Restoration in 1660 and returned to its status as the High Kirk of St Giles at the Glorious Revolution of 1689.) 1633 also saw the foundation of the Tron Kirk, designed by John Mylne, by the public weighing-beam about midway between St Giles and the Netherbow Port. The building of Parliament House, just south of St Giles's, to house the Scottish Parliament was begun in 1632 and completed in 1639. This was the time when the English traveller Sir William Brereton visited Edinburgh.

After the young Charles II's acceptance of the demands of the Covenanters in 1649, the Scottish army under David Leslie switched sides to support the royalist cause against Cromwell, by whom they were totally defeated at the Battle of Dunbar in 1650. Cromwell entered Edinburgh on 7 September of that year, four days after the battle. His troops did considerable damage to the city, destroying some of the churches (including Lady Yester's Kirk, built in 1644) and the High School, and causing a disastrous fire at Holyroodhouse where they were quartered. Cromwell later restored Holyrood, in an inferior style. In 1654, after General Monck's completion of the Cromwellian conquest of Scotland, England, Scotland and Ireland were united in a Commonwealth which lasted until the Restoration of 1660.

Political and religious controversy continued in Scotland and in Edinburgh from the Restoration until the Glorious Revolution of 1689, with continued Government attacks on the Covenanters and violent debates about religion. But this was also a time of cultural growth in Edinburgh. The very man who harried the Covenanters (who called him 'Bluidy Mackenzie'), Sir George Mackenzie of Rosehaugh, put Scots law on a new footing with his *Discourse on the Law and Customs of Scotland in*

Matters Criminal in 1674 and this in turn helped to make Edinburgh the great legal centre it became in the next century. Mackenzie also founded the Advocates' Library in Edinburgh (now the National Library of Scotland), and wrote works of fiction and philosophy. James Dalrymple, first Viscount Stair, made an even greater contribution to the provision of a coherent system and philosophy for Scots law in his *Institutions of the Law of Scotland* (1671) known to generations of law students in Scotland. It was at this time, too, that Edinburgh emerged as a centre of medical studies. In 1667 Sir Robert Sibbald and Dr Andrew Balfour founded the Physic Garden for which the magistrates provided part of the garden of Trinity Hospital (founded in the late fifteenth century on the site of the present Waverley Station): this later became the Royal Botanic Garden, now situated in the north of the city. Its head gardener was the botanist James Sutherland, who later became Edinburgh University's first professor of botany. In 1685 Sibbald became the first professor of medicine at Edinburgh, and together with Balfour and others, founded the Royal College of Physicians in the city in 1681. Edinburgh went on in the eighteenth century to become one of the great medical centres of the world.

If 1603 brought a change in the status of Edinburgh with the departure of the royal court, 1707 – the year in which the Scottish Parliament voted for an incorporating union with England – brought an even more momentous change. Edinburgh would no longer have a Parliament of its own sitting in Edinburgh, with its ceremonial 'riding' preceding the opening, but henceforth Scottish members would sit as a permanent minority in the Parliament at Westminster. Many unionists believed that the names of both Scotland and England would disappear, and Scotland would become 'North Britain'. Throughout the eighteenth century, and later, a considerable number of people, both Scots and English, did call Scotland 'North Britain', although almost nobody called England 'South Britain'. But the problem was more than a matter of nomenclature. What was the nature of Scottish identity after the Union and what was the character and function of its capital city, Edinburgh? The Union left Scotland with three elements unchanged: its religion, its legal establishment, and its educational system. The law and the church took over, in some respects, the guardianship of Scottish nationhood, and in Edinburgh especially, home of the Court of Session and the High Court of Justiciary, men of law were leaders of opinion. Historians, philosophers, literary critics, even agricultural improvers were more often than not trained in Scots law, and the advocates (Scottish equivalent of the English barristers) of Edinburgh were the social élite of the city. The prestige of law in Edinburgh lasted into the nineteenth century and beyond: both Walter Scott and Robert Louis Stevenson, Edinburgh men, were trained in the law and became advocates. As for the Church of Scotland, the burden of carrying a sense of Scottish nationhood proved hard, and splits and secessions developed as different groups claimed to speak for the religious conscience of the nation. But in Edinburgh the rise of Moderatism, a genteel form of humane Christianity that abandoned the harsher tenets of Calvinism, went hand in hand with a remarkable efflorescence of cultural life. The beginning of this efflorescence may be traced to the latter part of the seventeenth century, but the second half of the eighteenth century produced something much more remarkable than anything earlier.

This was the Scottish Enlightenment, which was not confined to Edinburgh (Glasgow played a significant part, and Aberdeen hardly less) but which flourished more richly in Edinburgh than elsewhere. The men of the Enlightenment, the *literati* as they liked to call themselves in Edinburgh, for the most part accepted the Union and thought of themselves as British as well as Scots. They were both proud of being Scots and eager to show that Scotland could demonstrate British intellectual life at its best. They made Edinburgh famous as an intellectual centre in Europe and America. David Hume, the greatest philosopher of his time and one of the greatest of any time; Adam Smith, the founder of Political Economy; William Cullen, physicist, chemist and pioneer in medical research and teaching; James Hutton, the founder of modern geology; Joseph Black, the distinguished chemist; William Robertson, the founder of modern historiography; Henry Home, Lord Kames, jurist, literary critic, philosopher, and agricultural improver; Lord Monboddo, philosopher, judge, anthropologist – these are only some of the distinguished names associated with the Scottish Enlighten- ment. In almost every area of human endeavour the aim was *improvement* – improvement of man's understanding of his own mind and body; of the nature of human society, its modes of developing and changing, and its cultural products; improve- ment in man's understanding of the natural world; improve- ment in ways of doing things that would increase human welfare and comfort.

It was under the influence of the ideals of the Scottish Enlightenment that civic improvement was undertaken in Edinburgh in the latter half of the eighteenth century. The expansion of the city was first to the south, with the laying out of George Square (where Walter Scott grew up) in 1766, of Buccleuch Street and Buccleuch Place in the 1770s, of Nicolson Street and Nicolson Square a decade earlier. These and adjacent streets represented a vernacular classical style, very much an Edinburgh style, while the succeeding development to the north (the New Town, as it came to be called) represented a more international and more consciously elegant and 'improving' classical style.

The improvement of Edinburgh was inspired largely by George Drummond, six times Lord Provost of the city between 1725 and 1764, and it was under his inspiration that a pamphlet entitled *Proposals for carrying on certain Public Works in the City of Edinburgh* was produced, probably by Sir Gilbert Elliott of Minto, in 1752. At first the site of new building was in the Old Town: the Royal Exchange was begun in the High Street in 1753, with John Adam as architect (it became the City Chambers in 1811), St Cecilia's Hall was built in 1763 as a concert hall at the corner of the Cowgate and of Niddry's Wynd that ran between the Cowgate and the High Street – it was modelled on the opera house at Parma and built by Robert Mylne, of the distinguished family of masons and architects, and restored by Edinburgh University in 1960.

But the most significant development went on to the north, after the draining of the Nor' Loch in the 1760s and the building

Edenborrow. Edenburgum. 1650 – a print copied from an original by
the Dutch artist, Rombout van den Hoyen

of the North Bridge, completed in 1772, that spanned the valley
dividing the Old Town from what was developing as the New
Town. In 1767 James Craig won the gold medal offered by the
Magistrates and Town Council of Edinburgh for the best plan of
the New Town. The plan, and the resulting streets and squares
(although they did not conform precisely to Craig's plan), were

monuments to the ideals of the Scottish Enlightenment. Order, elegance, rationality, improvement, were symbolized by the parallel streets, the matching squares, the quietly classical architecture of the buildings.

The New Town developed in stages. In 1789 the South Bridge, spanning the Cowgate valley south of the North Bridge, was completed: in the same year the new University building, designed by Robert Adam, was begun. These developments, however, were south of the High Street and the Old Town, and the essential New Town was to the north. Robert Reid and William Sibbald laid out the second phase of the New Town north of Queen Street: it included Heriot Row, where R.L. Stevenson grew up. Later developments produced terraces at the foot of Calton Hill. The hill itself, which was compared to the Acropolis at Athens, encouraged classical buildings, including the unfinished national monument to those who fell in the Napoleonic wars. It was in the early nineteenth century that Edinburgh began to be called the Athens of the North.

Developments at the west end of the city, by the Glasgow approaches, further enlarged the New Town, and finally the first New Town and later phases were connected with the valley of the Water of Leith to the north-west. The opening of Thomas Telford's spectacular Dean Bridge in 1831 produced easy access to the north and completed the Georgian development of the city.

So there was the Old Town, remaining for centuries within its original boundaries; first extensions to the south, including the vernacular classical George Square and its environs; the New Town to the north, made possible by bridging the valley and developing in several stages; and then came Victorian expansion between the Meadows and Blackford Hill, respectable middle class streets becoming more spacious as one moved south towards the hill. The coming of the railway brought significant changes, with a deep cutting under the foot of the Castle Rock from Waverley station in the east to the tunnel leading to Haymarket Station in the west. Considerable care was taken to preserve the city's amenities in the face of the railways running into and out of the city: a host of developments in the neighbourhood of Waverley Station and just south of the High Street produced Cockburn Street (1860), Victoria Street (1840) and George IV Bridge (1836), resulting in an interesting pattern of streets and buildings very near the centre of the Old Town. In general, however, Edinburgh to this day is 'a sort of three distinct cities', in the words of Robert Forsyth at the beginning of the nineteenth century – the Old Town, the New Town to the north, and the south side.

Leith, Edinburgh's seaport north of the city on the Firth of Forth, was granted to the burgh of Edinburgh in a charter of Robert the Bruce in 1329. This grant started a quarrel between independent minded Leithers and the city of Edinburgh which continued until the City Agreement Act of 1838 made Leith a separate municipality. But Leith, together with Granton and many other neighbouring villages and areas, was finally merged in Edinburgh by the Edinburgh Boundaries Extension Act of 1920.

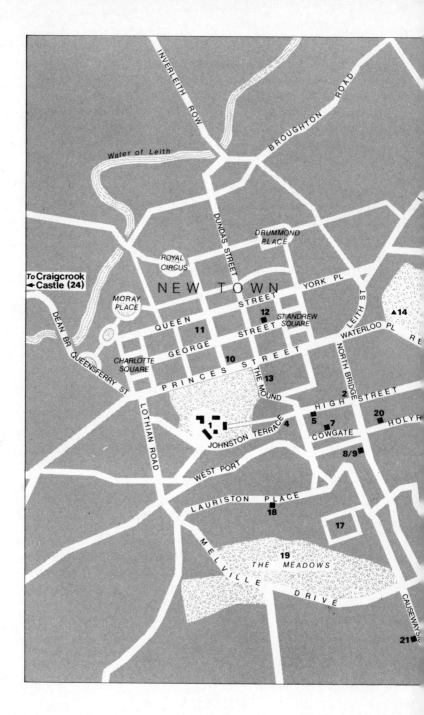

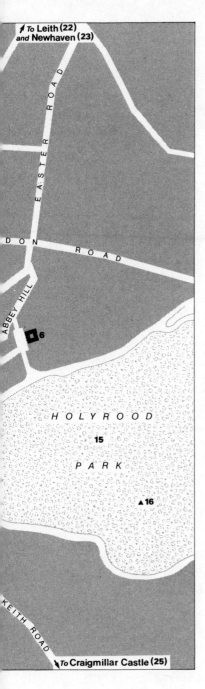

Map of the city
locating the places described

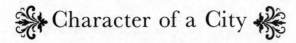# Character of a City

[1] The shape of the city; from *The Beauties of Scotland* by Robert Forsyth.

(Robert Forsyth was an Edinburgh advocate and miscellaneous writer whose five-volume *Beauties of Scotland*, published in 1805, provides a comprehensive account of the economic, social and physical characteristics of Scotland's cities and countryside.)

In consequence of its being divided in the way now mentioned, into a sort of three distinct cities, built upon separate parallel eminences, divided from each other by intervening valleys, there is no city of its extent less perplexing to a stranger, or where he is less likely to lose his way, than Edinburgh.

[2] A first view of the city in 1819; from *Peter's Letters to his Kinsfolk* by J.G. Lockhart.

(Lockhart was Sir Walter Scott's son-in-law and biographer.)

I know no city, where the lofty feelings, generated by the ideas of antiquity, and the multitude of human beings, are so much swelled and improved by the admixture of those other lofty, perhaps yet loftier feelings, which arise from the contemplation of free and spacious nature herself. Edinburgh, even were its population as great as that of London, could never be merely a city. Here there must always be present the idea of the comparative littleness of all human works. Here the proudest of palaces must be content to catch the shadows of mountains; and the grandest of fortresses to appear like the dwellings of pygmies, perched on the very bulwarks of creation. Everywhere – all around – you have rocks frowning over rocks in imperial elevation, and descending, among the smoke and dust of a city, into dark depths such as nature alone can excavate. The builders of the old city, too, appear as if they had made nature the model of their architecture. Seen through the lowering mist which almost perpetually envelopes them the huge masses of these erections, so high, so rugged in their outlines, so heaped together,

and conglomerated and wedged into each other, are not easily to
be distinguished from the yet larger and bolder forms of cliff and
ravine, among which their foundations have been pitched.
There is a certain gloomy indistinctness in the formation of these
fantastic piles, which leaves the eye, that would scrutinize and
penetrate them, unsatisfied and dim with gazing.

In company with the first friend I saw (of whom more anon), I
proceeded at once to take a look at this superb city from a height
placed just over the point where the old and new parts of the
town meet. These two quarters of the city, or rather these two
neighbouring but distinct cities, are separated by a deep green
valley, which once contained a lake, and which is now crossed at
one place by a huge earthen mound, and at another by a
magnificent bridge of three arches. This valley runs off towards
the estuary of the Forth, which lies about a mile and a half from
the city, and between the city and the sea there rises on each side
of it a hill – to the south called Arthur's Seat –to the north the
lower and yet sufficiently commanding eminence on which I
now stood – the Calton Hill.

This hill, which rises about 350 feet above the level of the sea,
is, in fact, nothing more than a huge pile of rocks covered with a
thin coating of soil, and, for the most part, with a beautiful
verdure. It has lately been circled all round with spacious
gravelled walks, so that one reaches the summit without the least
fatigue. It seems as if you had not quitted the streets, so easy is the
ascent; and yet where did streets or city ever afford such a
prospect! The view changes every moment as you proceed; yet
what grandeur of unity in the general and ultimate impression!
At first, you see only the skirts of the New Town, with apparently
few public edifices, to diversify the grand uniformity of their
outlines; then you have a rich plain, with green fields, groves,
and villas, gradually losing itself in the sea-port town of
Edinburgh – Leith. Leith covers, for a brief space, the margin of
that magnificent Frith, which recedes upwards among an
amphitheatre of mountains, and opens downward into the
ocean, broken everywhere by isles green and smiling, excepting
where the bare brown rock of the Bass lifts itself above the waters
midway to the sea. As you move round, the Frith disappears, and

you have Arthur's Seat in your front. In the valley between lies Holyrood, ruined – desolate – but majestic in its desolation. From thence the Old Town stretches its dark shadow – up, in a line to the summit of the Castle rock – a royal residence at either extremity – and all between an indistinguishable mass of black tower-like structures – the concentrated 'walled city', which has stood more sieges than I can tell of.

Here we paused for a time, enjoying the majestic gloom of this most picturesque of cities. A thick blue smoke hung low upon the houses, and their outlines reposed behind on ridges of purple clouds; – the smoke, and the clouds, and the murky air, giving yet more extravagant bulk and altitude to those huge strange dwellings, and increasing the power of contrast which met our view, when a few paces more brought us once again upon the New Town – the airy bridge – the bright green vale below and beyond it – and skirting the line of the vale an either side, the rough crags of the Castle rock, and the broad glare of Prince's Street, that most superb of terraces – all beaming in the open yellow light of the sun – steeples and towers, and cupolas scattered bright beneath our feet – and, as far as the eye could reach, the whole pomp and richness of distant commotion – the heart of the city.

Such was my first view of Edinburgh. I descended again into her streets in a sort of stupor of admiration.

[3] The buildings of Edinburgh in 1829; from *Modern Athens, Displayed in a Series of Views of Edinburgh in the Nineteenth Century, from Original Drawings by Mr Thomas H. Shepherd*, text by John Britton.

(John Britton was a London antiquary and topographer.)

The buildings of Edinburgh are dispersed over a very irregular surface of ground, and placed partly in valleys, and partly on the tops and sloping sides of hills. In the middle of the Old Town they are mostly arranged on the sides of narrow streets, are very high, and constructed without the least regard to symmetry, beauty, or domestic comforts. The New Town is as unlike its ancestor, as if belonging to another country, climate, or class of inhabitants; for whilst the former has no pretensions to beauty, or even architectural design – the latter is systematic, laid out with some regard to general effect, and according to an uniform and well-digested plan. It also exhibits several specimens of good architecture in its public buildings and private houses, that emulate the classical models of Italy. This may be inferred from the names of Sir William Chambers, and of the Adams's, who gave the designs for some of these edifices. Wide streets, laid out at right angles with each other, and terminated occasionally by spacious and handsome squares, give an air of beauty, and even of grandeur, to parts of this newly-formed district. In these features it may be said to resemble the famed city of Washington, in America. Built on an eminence, about 200 feet above the level of the sea, and considerably above the Old Town, it not only commands varied and extensive prospects, but is seen towering above the low grounds in the vicinity. At its western side the surface shelves abruptly to a small river called the Water of Leith; whilst near the eastern extremity, is a lofty, craggy, insulated eminence, called the Calton Hill.

The Northern district of Edinburgh, generally called the *New Town*, was first projected in 1752, but as the magistrates were at that time unable to procure an extension of the royalty, the design was postponed until the year 1767, when an act of parliament was obtained, by which they were empowered to effect this important object. It was at first proposed to make a canal through the North Loch, and to lay out the northern bank in terraces: this process was partially adopted; and was carrying into effect when Provost Drummond devised a scheme for draining the Loch, and to occupying the hollow by throwing across the North-Bridge, and thereby forming a communication with a large level space of ground, the property of Heriot's Hospital. This plan was acted upon, and the New Town was, contrary to every prediction on the subject, built and occupied, to a considerable extent, within forty years from its commencement. The district may be considered as consisting of two parts, the one begun in 1767 and now completed; and the other, the additional buildings erected to the north, east, and west of the former. The principal avenue in the New Town is George-street, which extends through the centre, and is terminated at the east end by St Andrew's Square, in the centre of which, stands a handsome column, erected to the memory of the late Lord Melville. At the west end of the same street is another quadrangular area, called Charlotte Square, surrounded by large and respectable mansions. In a recess on the eastern side of St Andrew's Square, is the *Royal Bank*, formerly the Excise Office, a handsome building, designed by Sir William Chambers; close to which is situated the *British Linen Bank*. On the west side of Charlotte Square, is *St George's Church*, forming the terminating object of George-street. Parallel to this street, are Queen-street, Princes-street, and York Place; at the eastern end of the former is St Paul's Chapel, built by a subscription of the members of the Scottish Episcopal Church, from a design by Archibald Elliot, Esq. At the western termination of Princes-street is St John's Chapel, a light building, also erected by subscription: and at the eastern end of the same street stands the *Theatre*, immediately opposite to which is the *Register Office*, erected from a design by Mr Robert Adam, the foundation-stone of which was laid on the 7th of June, 1774. There are also two other longitudinal streets, named Thistle-street, and Rose-street, the former running between Queen-street and George-street, and the latter between Princes-street and George-street.

[4] Looking back on the 1860s; from *Memoirs of Two Cities, Edinburgh and Aberdeen* by David Masson.

(Masson was Professor of English at Edinburgh University from 1865 until 1895.)

Always one of the first views, on approaching the city from a particular quarter, was that which gave you, once for all, the bold, romantic outlines of the whole – the high, rock-rounding Castle on one side, the monumented Acropolis of the Calton Hill on the other, the ridgy mass of building between, and behind all,

the noble shoulder and peak of Arthur Seat, and the great
scarped curve of Salisbury Crags. This was a view repeated again
and again, with variations, in a thousand subsequent walks
about the suburbs, till Arthur Seat became to you, not from one
point but from many, actually that couchant lion keeping guard
over the city into which the local myth had interpreted its form.
Next after this view in frequency, if not the most frequent view of
all after you were a denizen of the city, was the interior view in
the walk along Princes Street. Walking along this street – which
you could not but do twice or thrice every day – you were in the
bisecting valley between the New Town and the Old; and if your
course was eastward, you had on your right the grassy steeps of
the Castle-rock, and then the quaint, dense, sky-serrated mass of
tall, many-storeyed old houses, the main Edinburgh of the past,
which detaching itself from the Castle, with the name of the High
Street, descends, as the Canongate, towards Holyrood Abbey
and the Palace. It was a walk in which you always lingered, with
a view varying as it was morning or evening, sunlight or grey
weather, and of which you never tired.

  Then, if you took but a few steps out of Princes Street, by the
open way, called the Mound, leading up to the Old Town, and
from that partial elevation stopped to look westward, what a
change in the panorama! You were in the heart of a city, and yet,
lo! both near at hand and afar off, a sylvan land – closest of all to
the city the softly-wooded Corstorphine Hills, and, beside and
beyond them, expanses dying to distant beginnings of mountains
and a horizon of faint amethyst. Perhaps you completed the
ascent into the Old Town, and, turning up the High Street to the
Castle esplanade, passed the portcullised gateway over the dry
moat, and threaded the rocky and winding path within the gate,
amid the lounging soldiers and pacing sentries of the garrison, till
you came out on the highest battlements beside huge superannu-
ated Mons Meg and the inferior modern cannons to which she
has resigned her duty. From that magnificent station in the high
cool air you would gaze, it might be for half an hour or more,
northwards, northwards and all around. What a grand range of
survey! Beneath you, paralleled and rectangled over a succession
of slopes, the whole of the new city and its gardens, so that the
cannon from where you stood could blast it into ruins at a

descending angle, and so that always, when they do fire on peaceful gala-days, the windows of the city rattle and shiver with the far-going reverberation; beyond this city the villa studded banks of the Forth; again beyond these the Firth's own flashing waters; and, still beyond even these, the towns, villages, and heights of the opposite Fifeshire coast. On either side, too, with scarce a turn of the head, other views for many a league, till you could make out, on a clear day, that the risings in the amethystine distance to your left were really the summits of the far Highland mountains.

If, instead of the Castle, it was the Calton Hill that you favoured – and to walk round the Calton Hill was a matter of course in any five minutes of spare time that might happen thereabouts – there was something of the same vastness in the *ensemble* but with much of sea-change. Sea-change, I say; for, though from one part of this walk round the Hill there was a perspective of the line of Princes Street and of the main adjacent city, and from another there was the finest view of Holyrood down in its valley and of Arthur Seat rising behind, what ravished one through the main part of the circuit was the Firth and its shores – the Firth, either widening out to the open sea-haze between Fife-Ness and North Berwick Law, and showing through the haze the dim shapes of islands and headlands, and of bays beyond dusky Leith, brick-coned Portobello, and the other near coast-towns, or else winding and narrowing more clearly inland to where, over a maze of streets and chimney-stacks crowded under the very base of the hill, the sites of Burntisland, Aberdour, Inverkeithing, and the other coast-towns of Fife, directly opposite to Edinburgh, seemed so definite as to be within arm's hail or other friendly signal. For this characteristic sight, however, of the Firth's waters and the Fifeshire coast from the very heart of Edinburgh, you did not need to ascend any height. Walking in George Street, the next parallel of the New Town to Princes Street, there, at every gap or crossing, you had the same vision of the Firth and of the far Fifeshire coast flashed momentarily upon you; and, if you descended one of those cross-streets, leading down the well-gardened declivity, the vision was permanent.

But why attempt an inventory of the endless points of view,

within or close by Edinburgh, where the power of its manifold attractions made itself felt? Descend to its old Grassmarket and look up thence at one end of the great Castle on its most lofty and precipitous side; dive down its Canongate, or place yourself wherever else, deep amid the old and tall houses, you were most shut in from air and open view in any direction except overhead – there, not the less for all the squalor of the social degeneracy that now tenants these localities, there was still the abounding picturesque. Pass to the opener and newer parts of the city, and everywhere, despite drawbacks, there was richness of new effect. Widen your range and again circumambulate the suburbs, and you enclosed, as it were, all the interest now accumulated for you on the built space within a circumference of interest equally detailed and various.

Finally, to ring in the whole imaginatively, and partly to sever the aggregate Edinburgh you knew from the surrounding country, partly to connect it wherewith, there were the walks and excursions that could be taken on any vacant afternoon. Of these – whether for the geologist (for whom the whole vicinity of Edinburgh is specially rich in instruction) or for the pedestrian of vaguer natural tastes – there was great variety of choice. You might climb Arthur Seat by the shoulder or the peak, or you might round the curve of Salisbury Crags, and so find yourself, on the other side, on the quiet edge of Duddingston loch and village, beautiful themselves, and with miles of southern quietude and beauty beyond. The easiest amount of persistence from where you then were, by pleasant roads and past quaint villages, would take you to the celebrated loveliness of Roslin, and the fairy haunts of Hawthornden. Or, starting through one part of the Old Town, by way of the Meadows and Bruntsfield Links, you came, by Merchiston Castle, to sunny Morningside, whence before you lay the Braid Hills and the great brown range of the larger Pentlands; and so, past the Braid Hills, till you did gain the Pentlands and were footing, out of ken of man, and with quickened climber's breath, a wilderness of glorious moor.

Or, choosing another direction, and taking Dean Bridge over the great dell of the Water of Leith from the west end of the town, you might follow the wide Queensferry Road, with open views all the way, as far as Craigleith Quarry, where, down in a vast hole, the depth of which from its precipitous edges made you dizzy, you heard the clank of hammers on iron, and saw horses and carts moving, and, here and there, men blasting the freestone; or, if you deviated from the main Queensferry Road into the quieter and narrow road parallel to it on the left, you might have a sweeter walk still by the lovely woods and houses of Ravelston, sheltered inimitably in their exquisite nook, and might thence continue to turreted Craigcrook, antique in its grounds of roses and evergreens, or lose yourself, above Craigcrook, among the soft heights of the protecting Corstorphines. . . .

In all towns and cities, be they what they like during the day, the nocturnal aspects are impressive. Night flings her mantle over the mean; and, wherever, even on the flattest ground, there are piles of building, or objects in blocks, with gaps of intersection, she plays among these a poesy of her own in endless phantasies of dark and silver. But Edinburgh, by reason of her heights and hollows, invests herself at night more wondrously than any city I have seen with this mystery of the vast terrestial shadow struggling below with the lurid artifice of lamps, or star-pierced from above till it yields in azure. What a spectacle is that of the ordinary walk along Princes Street at night, when the windows of the Old Town are lit, and across the separating chasm there looms darkly, or is seen more clearly, the high, continuous cliff of gables, irregularly brilliant with points of radiance!

[5] The windy city, 1878; from *Edinburgh, Picturesque Notes* by Robert Louis Stevenson.

The ancient and famous metropolis of the North sits overlooking a windy estuary from the slope and summit of three hills. No situation could be more commanding for the head city of a kingdom; none better chosen for noble prospects. From her tall precipice and terraced gardens she looks far and wide on the sea and broad champaigns. To the east you may catch at sunset the

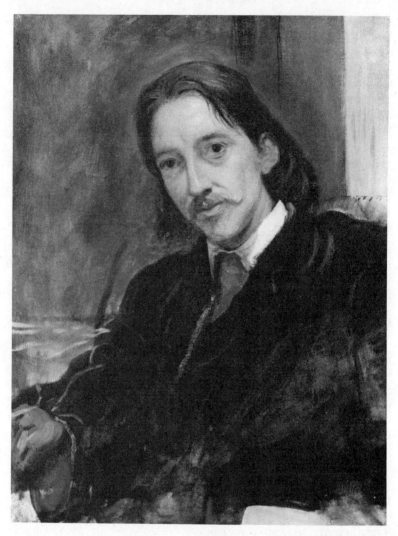

Robert Louis Stevenson, 1887; by W.B. Richmond

spark of the May lighthouse, where the Firth expands into the German Ocean; and away to the west, over all the carse of Stirling, you can see the first snows upon Ben Ledi.

But Edinburgh pays cruelly for her high seat in one of the vilest climates under the heaven. She is liable to be beaten upon by all the winds that blow, to be drenched with rain, to be buried in cold sea fogs out of the east, and powdered with the snow as it comes flying southward from the Highland hills. The weather is raw and boisterous in winter, shifty and ungenial in summer, and downright meteorological purgatory in the spring. The delicate die early, and I, as a survivor, among bleak winds and plumping rain, have been sometimes tempted to envy them their fate. For all who love shelter and the blessings of the sun, who hate dark weather and perpetual tilting against squalls, there could scarcely be found a more unhomely and harassing place of residence. Many such aspire angrily after that Somewhere-else of the imagination, where all troubles are supposed to end. They lean over the great bridge which joins the New Town with the Old – and watch the trains smoking out from under them and vanishing into the tunnel on a voyage to brighter skies. Happy the passengers who shake off the dust of Edinburgh, and have heard for the last time the cry of the east wind among her chimney-tops! And yet the place establishes an interest in people's hearts; go where they will, they find no city of the same distinction; go where they will, they take a pride in their old home.

Venice, it has been said, differs from all other cities in the sentiment which she inspires. The rest may have admirers; she only, a famous fair one, counts lovers in her train. And indeed, even by her kindest friends, Edinburgh is not considered in a similar sense. These like her for many reasons, not any one of which is satisfactory in itself. They like her whimsically, if you will, and somewhat as a virtuoso dotes upon his cabinet. Her attraction is romantic in the narrowest meaning of that term. Beautiful as she is, she is not so much beautiful as interesting. She is pre-eminently Gothic, and all the more so since she has set herself off with some Greek airs, and erected classic temples on her crags. In a word, and above all, she is a curiosity. . . .

Again, meditative people will find a charm in a certain consonancy between the aspect of the city and its odd and stirring history. Few places, if any, offer a more barbaric display of contrasts to the eye. In the very midst stands one of the most satisfactory crags in nature – a Bass Rock upon dry land rooted in a garden shaken by passing trains, carrying a crown of battlements and turrets, and describing its warlike shadow over the liveliest and brightest thoroughfare of the new town. From their smoky beehives, ten stories high, the unwashed look down upon the open squares and gardens of the wealthy; and gay people sunning themselves along Princes Street, with its mile of commercial palaces all beflagged upon some great occasion, see, across a gardened valley set with statues, where the washings of the old town flutter in the breeze at its high windows. And then, upon all sides, what a clashing of architecture! In this one valley, where the life of the town goes busily forward, there may be seen, shown one above and behind another by the accidents of the ground, buildings in almost every style upon the globe. Egyptian and Greek temples, Venetian palaces and Gothic spires, are huddled one over another in a most admired disorder; while, above all, the brute mass of the Castle and the summit of Arthur's Seat look down upon these imitations with a becoming dignity, as the works of Nature may look down upon the monuments of Art. But Nature is a more indiscriminate patroness than we imagine, and in no way frightened of a strong effect. The birds roost as willingly among the Corinthian capitals as in the crannies of the crag; the same atmosphere and daylight clothe the eternal rock and yesterday's imitation portico; and as the soft northern sunshine throws out everything into a glorified distinctness – or easterly mists, coming up with the blue evening, fuse all these incongruous features into one, and the lamps begin to glitter across the street, and faint lights to burn in the high windows across the valley – the feeling grows upon you that this also is a piece of nature in the most intimate sense; that this profusion of eccentricities, this dream in masonry and living rock is not a drop-scene in a theatre, but a city in the world of everyday reality, connected by railway and telegraph-wire with all the capitals of Europe, and inhabited by citizens of the

familiar type, who keep ledgers, and attend church, and have
sold their immortal portion to a daily paper. By all the canons of
romance, the place demands to be half-deserted and leaning
towards decay; birds we might admit in profusion, the play of the
sun and winds, and a few gypsies encamped in the chief
thoroughfare; but these citizens with their cabs and their
tramways, their trains and posters, are altogether out of key.
Chartered tourists, they make free with historic localities, and
rear their young among the most picturesque sights with a grand
human indifference. To see them thronging by, in their neat
clothes and conscious moral rectitude, and with a little air of
possession that verges on the absurd, is not the least striking
feature of the place.

[6] Looking back on the 1920s; from *Was: A Pastime from
Time Past* by David Daiches.

Stories should be tailored to the suggestions of particular places.
How different for example was Arthur's Seat from Blackford
Hill, Leith from Portobello, even Bruntsfield Links from the
Meadows. As for the Castle, brooding over the city, it was too
much always there, too permanent and accepted and matter-of-
course a feature of the skyline to arouse romantic suggestions.
Did Morningside suggest Lucifer son of the morning? By no
means. It was genteel and intimate and pleasantly ordinary,
decent and friendly and unadventurously urban, with flats and
houses from which issued every morning solicitors and school-
masters and branch managers of banks. But somewhere in
Morningside there was a lunatic asylum – he had never seen it –
and the name was used familiarly to suggest the place where mad
people were sent. Quite daft, he ought to be sent to Morningside,
they would say at school. Yet the word had no connection with
the visible and agreeable ordinariness of Morningside Road and
the respectable streets that went off it at right angles. Tollcross
was the sentinel guarding the divisions; from there you went east
by Lauriston past the back of his school and of the Royal
Infirmary and near the Graham Street synagogue and past

Heriot's to where the Middle Meadow Walk came in opposite
Forrest Road; or south-east by Brougham Place to Melville
Drive and the south side of the Meadows, his own much
frequented territory; or south through Bruntsfield and
Morningside to the Braid Hills; or south-west by Craiglockhart
and Colinton to the Pentlands; or north down Lothian Road to
the West End. What diversity, what richness, innumerable cities
in one, country places and metropolitan streets flowing into each
other. From the West End you could get a tramcar to
Murrayfield, and from the car terminus a tiny little bus ran to the
zoo at Corstorphine. He would lie in bed and make journeys in
his head, changing the feeling with each district, imagining
suitable characters and adventures. There was a little tailor's
shop in Polwarth Terrace, on the way to Craiglockhart, where
he got his first suit with long trousers, fitted by a sad man with a
thick moustache, a little shop, a little sad tailor, with no other
customers that he could see and an air of desperately trying to
make good as something more than a little sad tailor's shop.
What was such a man doing trapped between Craiglockhart and
Tollcross, a doomed tailor surely, with crossed ambitions and
strange inner thoughts? The suit with the long trousers was
greeny-grey, reminiscent of the tailor, the shop, the sadness.

'Southward of Morningside lie the Plewlands, ascending the
slope towards beautiful Craiglockhart Hill, now being fast
covered with semi-detached villas, feued by the Scottish Heri-
tages Company, surrounding a new cemetery, and intersected
by the suburban line of railway.' That was the voice of the
Edinburgh historian of the 1870s, and those semi-detached villas
were now solidly entrenched as a quietly determined part of
southern Edinburgh respectabilities. As for the suburban line of
railway, he knew best the stretch between Newington and
Blackford Hill and had often watched the trains from Blackford
Hill or from where Oswald Road went over the railway line as
they puffed in their suburban circle round the city. Goods trains
went on the line at night, and often on a still night he could hear
the puff puff puffing of an engine and sometimes from further
distance borne the lonely whistle of a night express going east
then south from Waverley. These sounds did not carry in the

daytime; only when the rest of the city was still could he hear the puffs and the whistles and sometimes even the distant clanking of trucks knocking against each other. Mysterious and beautiful noises they were, indicating adventurous nocturnal activity. Passenger trains at night, their moving windows lit up, had a special fascination, and when he heard the whistle crying in the darkness he imagined the travellers sitting in their lighted boxes being carried through the surrounding black and the engine driver, his face lit up by the fire, watching for the lights at the corner of the signals as he drove his train through the deserted nightscape. But the suburban passenger trains went only during the day, and chugged unadventurously along on their douce daily rounds.

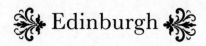 Edinburgh

The Castle

[7] The recapture of Edinburgh Castle from the English in March 1313; from *Tales of a Grandfather* by Sir Walter Scott.

(This exploit is described (from authentic traditions) in John Barbour's late fourteenth-century poem 'The Bruce': Barbour's fourteenth-century Scots is difficult for the modern reader, so Sir Walter Scott's account, which is based on Barbour, has been chosen instead.)

While Robert Bruce was gradually getting possession of the country, and driving out the English, Edinburgh, the principal town of Scotland, remained with its strong castle, in possession of the invaders. Sir Thomas Randolph was extremely desirous to gain this important place; but, as you well know, the castle is situated on a very steep and lofty rock, so that it is difficult or almost impossible even to get up to the foot of the walls, much more to climb over them.

So while Randolph was considering what was to be done, there came to him a Scottish gentleman, named Francis, who had joined Bruce's standard, and asked to speak with him in private. He then told Randolph, that in his youth he had lived in the castle of Edinburgh, and that his father had then been keeper of the fortress. It happened at that time that Francis was much in love with a lady, who lived in a part of the town beneath the castle, which is called the Grassmarket. Now, as he could not get out of the castle by day to see his mistress, he had practised a way of clambering by night down the castle rock on the south side, and returning at his pleasure; when he came to the foot of the wall, he made use of a ladder to get over it, as it was not very high at that point, those who built it having trusted to the steepness of the crag; and for the same reason, no watch was placed there. Francis had gone and come so frequently in this dangerous manner, that, though it was now long ago, he told Randolph he knew the road so well that he would undertake to guide a small party of men by night to the bottom of the wall; and as they might bring ladders with them, there would be no difficulty in scaling it. The great risk was, that of being discovered by the watchmen while in the act of ascending the cliff, in which case every man of them must have perished.

Nevertheless, Randolph did not hesitate to attempt the adventure. He took with him only thirty men (you may be sure they were chosen for activity and courage), and came one dark night to the foot of the rock, which they began to ascend under the guidance of Francis, who went before them, upon his hands and feet, up one cliff, down another, and round another, where there was scarce room to support themselves. All the while, these thirty men were obliged to follow in a line, one after the other, by a path that was fitter for a cat than a man. The noise of a stone falling, or a word spoken from one to another, would have alarmed the watchmen. They were obliged, therefore, to move with the greatest precaution. When they were far up the crag, and near the foundation of the wall, they heard the guards going their rounds, to see that all was safe in and about the castle. Randolph and his party had nothing for it but to lie close and quiet, each man under the crag, as he happened to be placed, and trust that the guards would pass by without noticing them. And while they were waiting in breathless alarm, they got a new cause of fright. One of the soldiers of the castle, willing to startle his comrades, suddenly threw a stone from the wall, and cried out, 'Aha, I see you well!' The stone came thundering down over the heads of Randolph and his men, who naturally thought themselves discovered. If they had stirred, or made the slightest noise, they would have been entirely destroyed; for the soldiers above might have killed every man of them, merely by rolling down stones. But being courageous and chosen men, they remained quiet, and the English soldiers, who thought their comrade was merely playing them a trick (as, indeed, he had no other meaning in what he did and said), passed on, without further examination.

Then Randolph and his men got up, and came in haste to the foot of the wall, which was not above twice a man's height in that place. They planted the ladders they had brought, and Francis mounted first to show them the way; Sir Andrew Grey, a brave knight, followed him, and Randolph himself was the third man who got over. Then the rest followed. When once they were within the walls, there was not so much to do, for the garrison were asleep and unarmed, excepting the watch, who were speedily destroyed. Thus was Edinburgh Castle taken in March, 1312–13.

[8] Rivalry among the great families of Scotland led to many acts of violence, notable among which was the killing of the young Earl of Douglas in the Castle in 1440; from *A General History of Scotland, Together with a Particular History of the Houses of Douglas and Angus* by David Hume of Godscroft.

(David Hume of Godscroft, c. 1560–1630, was Secretary of the eighth Earl of Angus.)

The Earl of Douglas was of the old spirit, of the ancient Nobilitie: he could not save, nor obey but whom he ought, and the lawfull commanders, lawfully commanding for his honour and utility, whereof they [his enemies] were neither. Such a spirit is unsufferable, under these new conspiring Tyrants: he will not acknowledge their authority, his father had told them their holy dayes name, himselfe tooke them for his enemies. But how shall they doe with him? hee is not easily to be dealt with, they must have muffles that would catch such a cat. ... And although he was but fourteen years of age at his father's death (in the year 1438 or 39) and was put to death in the year 1440 not having attained to fifteen or sixteen, or little above at the farthest, yet in this his part and behaviour, did not onely appeare the sparks of a great spirit, but also of such wisedome and providence as could scarce be looked for from so young a man. This galled them so much the more to thinke if that fruit should come to ripenesse at any time, how poysonable, or rather, how great a counterpoyse it would prove to their greatnesse. But here the skinne of the Lion

Prospect of the Castle and City of Edenborrow from the North Loch, by
Slezer, 1690. The Nor' Loch was drained in the 1760s, and Princes
Street Gardens now occupy the site

would not save their turne (he was too hard for them to deal with
by force) they do there sow on that of the Fox. . . .

Wherefore he [*Sir Alexander Levingston, one of the leaders of the
conspiracy against Douglas*] procured a letter to be written to him in
an honorable manner in all their names, intreating him, that
being mindful of his place, mindful of his Progenitours, whose
good deed and deservings, most ample and notable towards his
Countrey of Scotland, were still extant, he would come to the
Convention of the States, which could not be conveniently kept
without him, & his friends. . . .

This letter, as it was honest in words, and very right, carrying
that right course that should have been used towards him and
the duety that all these reasons contained, craved to have been
done to him, if it had been in sincerity: so being in falsehood, and

with a treacherous intention, used only to entrap him, makes their ditty the clearer: for he (out of the honesty of his owne heart) interpreting their meaning to be according to their words, and being of no ill disposition, but of a sweet and tractable nature, desirous of glory by good means, that so hee might have followed the footsteps of his Predecessours in all good offices to his Countrey, not having so great malice in his minde, and therefore not thinking any could have so great in theirs against him, as to take his life. . . . he willingly embraces the occasion of making peace in the Countrey, & that he might contribute there to his best endeavours, taketh his journey for Edinburgh. . . .

. . . However, this noble youth goeth in the innocencey of his heart . . . with his brother, and with a few other principall friends . . . directly to the Castle (being led and as it were drawne by a fatall destiny) and both enter, and so come in the power of those their deadly enemies and fained friends. . . . At last about the end of dinner, they compasse him about with armed men, and cause present a bulls head before him on the board: the bulls head was in those days a token of death. . . . The young Nobleman either understanding the signe as an ordinary thing, or astonished with it as an uncouth thing, upon the sight of the Bulls head offering to rise, was laid hold of by their armed men in the King's presence at the King's table, which should have been a Sanctuary to him. An so without regard of King, or any duty, and without any further processe, without order, assise (or jurie), no crime objected, he not being convicted at all; a young man of that age that was not liable to the law in regard of his youth, a Nobleman of that place, a worthy Gentleman of such expectation, a guest of that acceptation, one who had reposed upon their credit, who had committed himselfe to them, a friend in mind, who looked for friendship, to whom all friendship was promised; against dutie, law, friendship, faith, honesty, humanitie, hospitalitie; against nature, against humane society, against Gods Law, against mans law, and the law of nature, is cruelly executed, and put to death.

It is sore that the people did abhor it, execrating the very place where it was done, in detestation of the fact: of which the memory remaineth yet to our dayes in these words.

Edinburgh Castle, Towne and Tower,
God grant thou sinke for sinne;
And that even for the black dinner
Earle Douglas *got therein.*

[9] When Mary Queen of Scots fled to England in 1568, Scotland was governed by the Earl of Morton in the name of the child James VI; Sir William Kirkcaldy of Grange held Edinburgh Castle in the name of Queen Mary against Morton and the King's men, 1571–3; from *Old and New Edinburgh* by James Grant.

(James Grant, 1822–1887) was an Edinburgh architect who turned to literature and antiquities; he wrote novels as well as his massive three-volume work on Edinburgh.)

When joined by some English pioneers, Morton began to invest the Castle with his paid Scottish companies, who formed a battery on the Castle hill, from which Kirkaldy drove them all in rout on the night of the 15th. On the following day, Sir William Drury, in direct violation of the Treaty of Blois, which declared 'that no foreign troops should enter Scotland', at the head of the old bands of Berwick about 1,500 men, marched for Edinburgh. A trumpeter, on the 25th of April, summoned Kirkaldy to surrender; but he replied by hoisting, in place of the St Andrew's ensign, a red flag on David's Tower as a token of resistance to the last.

Five batteries had been erected against him by the 15th of May. These were armed with thirty guns, including two enormous bombardes or 100-pounders, which were loaded by means of a crane; a great carthoun or 48-pounder; and many 18-pounders. There was also a movable battery of falcons. . . .

All these guns opened simultaneously on Sunday, the 17th of May, by salvoes; and the shrieks of the women in the Castle were distinctly heard in the camp of the Regent and in the city. The fire was maintained on both sides with unabated vigour – nor were the arquebuses idle – till the 23rd, when Sutton's guns having breached David's Tower, the enormous mass, with all its guns and men, and with a roar as of thunder, came crashing over the rocks, and masses of it must have fallen into the loch 200 feet below. The Gate Tower with the portcullis and Wallace's Tower, were battered down by the 24th. The guns of the queen's garrison were nearly silenced now, and cries of despair were heard. The great square Peel and the Constable's Tower, with the curtain between, armed with brass cannon – edifices of great antiquity – came crashing down in succession, and their *débris* choked up the still existing draw-wells. Still the garrison did not quite lose heart, until the besiegers got possession of the Spur, within which was the well on which the besieged depended chiefly for water. This great battery then covered half of the Esplanade. Holinshed mentions another spring, St Margaret's Well, from which Kirkaldy's men secretly obtained water till the besiegers poisoned it! By this time the survivors were so exhausted by toil and want of food as to be scarcely able to bear armour, or work the remaining guns. On the 28th Kirkaldy requested a parley by beat of drum, and was lowered over the ruins by ropes in his armour, to arrange a capitulation; but Morton would hear of nothing now save an unconditional surrender, so the red flag of defiance was pulled down on the following day. By the Regent's order the Scottish companies occupied the breaches, with orders to exclude all Englishmen. The governor delivered his sword to Sir William Drury on receiving the solemn assurance of being restored to his estate and liberty at the intercession of Queen Elizabeth. The remnant of his garrison marched into the city in armour with banners displayed; there came forth, with the Lord Home, twelve knights, 100 soldiers, and ten boys, with several ladies, including the countess of Argyle. The brave commander was basely delivered up by Drury to the vindictive power of the Regent; and he and his brother Sir James, with two burgesses of the city, were drawn backwards in carts to the market cross, where they were hanged, and their heads were placed upon the ruined castle walls.

[10] The Castle in 1598; from *An Itinerary written by Fynes Moryson, gent.*

(Fynes Moryson was an Englishman who, after graduating from Cambridge, decided to 'gaine experience by travelling into forraigne parts'. He visited Edinburgh in 1598.)

At the farthest end towards the West, is a very strong Castle, which the Scots hold unexpugnable. *Camden* saith this castle was of old called by the Britaines, *Castle meyned agned*, by the Scots; the Castle of the Maids or Virgines (of certaine Virgines kept there for the Kings of the Picts), and by *Ptolemy* the winged Castle. And from this castle towards the West, is a most steepe Rocke pointed on the highest top, out of which this Castle is cut: But on the North and South sides without the walls, lie plaine and fruitfull fields of Corne.

[11] The Castle in 1618; from *The Pennyles Pilgrimage: or the money-less perambulation of John Taylor from London to Edenborough* by John Taylor.

(John Taylor, the 'water poet', Thames waterman as well as lively versifier and flamboyant prose writer, made a journey on foot from London to Scotland in 1618.)

The castle on a loftie rocke is so strongly grounded, bounded, and founded, that by force of man it can never be confounded; the foundation and walls are unpenetrable, the rampiers impregnable, the bulwarkes invincible, no way but one to it is or can be possible to be made passable. In a word, I have seene many straights and fortresses in Germany, the Netherlands, Spaine, and England, but they must all give place to this unconquered castle, both for strength and situation.

Amongst the many memorable things which I was shewed there, I noted especially a great peece of ordnance of iron[*this is the great gun known as Mons Meg, first referred to in 1488*]; it is not for batterie, but it will serve to defend a breach, or to tosse balles of wilde-fire against any that should assaile or assault the castle; it lyes now dismounted; and it is so great within, that it was told me that a childe was once gotten there: but I, to make tryall crept into it, lying on my backe, and I am sure there was roome enough and spare for a greater than my selfe.

[12] The Castle in 1636; from *The Diary of Sir William Brereton*.

(Sir William Brereton, from Cheshire, MP for Cheshire in 1628 and 1640, and Parliamentary Commander in the Civil War, visited Scotland in 1636.)

This *Saturday*, after dinner, I took a view of the castle here, which is seated very high and sufficiently commanding, and being able to batter the town; this is also seated upon the top of a most hard rock, and the passage whereunto was (as they there report) made through that hard and impregnable rock, which cannot be touched or hewed, and it is indeed a stately passage, wherein was used more industry, pains, art, and endeavour, than in any place I have found amongst the Scotts. It is but a very little castle, of no great receipt, but mighty strength; it is called Castrum Puellarum, because the kings of the Picts kept their virgins therein; upon the wall of the castle, towards the top, is this insculpsion, part thereof gilt – a crown and sceptre, and dagger placed under it cross-wise, with this super-scription:'Nobis haec invicta miserunt, 106 proavi'; the same arms and inscription is placed upon the front of the abbey, which is the king's house. Out of the court of this high-seated castle, there was one that watched (a soldier in his turn) in a little wooden house or cabin, which by a whirlwind was taken and thrown down both together over the castle wall and to the bottom of this high and steep rock, and the man not hurt or bruised, save only his finger put out of joint.

[13] The Castle in 1661: a French view; from the *Antiquarian Repertory*, Volume IV.

(Jorevin de Rocheford's account of his travels was published in Paris in 1672: this is the first English translation.)

Edenburgh is the capital town, and the handsomest of the kingdom of Scotland, distant only a mile from the sea, where Lith is its sea-port. It stands on a hill, which it entirely occupies. This hill, on the side whereon the castle is built, is scarped down as steep as a wall, which adds to its strength, as it is accessible only on one side, which is therefore doubly fortified with bastions, and a large ditch cut sloping into the rock. I arrived by the suburbs, at the foot of the castle where at the entry is the market-place, which forms the beginning of a great street in the lower town, called Couguet [Cowgate]. On coming into this place, one is first struck with the appearance of a handsome fountain, and, a little higher up, with the grand hospital or alms-house for the poor: there is no one but would at first sight take it for a palace. You ascend to it by a long staircase, which ends before a platform facing the entry at the great gate. The portico is supported by several columns, and the arms and stature of the founder, with a tablet of black marble, on which there is an inscription, signifying, that he was a very rich merchant, who died without children. There are four large pavilions, ornamented with little turrets, connected by four large wings, forming a square court in the middle, with galleries sustained by columns, serving for communications to the apartments of this great edifice. One might pass much time in considering the pieces of sculpture and engraving in these galleries, the magnitude of its chambers and halls, and the good order observed in this great hospital. Its garden is the walk and place of recreation for the citizens, but a stranger cannot be admitted without the introduction of some inhabitant. You will there see a bowling-green, as in many other places in England: it is a smooth even meadow, resembling a green carpet, a quantity of fruit-trees, and a well-kept kitchen-garden. . . .

I lodged at Edenburgh in the house of a French cook, who

directed me to the merchant on whom I had taken a bill of exchange at London. He took me into the castle, which one may call impregnable, on account of its situation, since it is elevated on a rock scarped on every side, except that which looks to the town, by which we entered after having passed the drawbridge, defended by a strong half-moon, where there is no want of cannon. This brings to my mind one seen in entering the court [*Mons Meg*], which is of so great a length and breadth, that two persons have laid in it as much at their ease as in a bed. The people of the castle tell a story of it more pleasant than true: they say it was made in order to carry to the port of Lyth against such enemies as might arrive by sea; we saw several of its bullets, of an almost immeasurable size.

[14] When Bonnie Prince Charlie and his Highland army occupied Edinburgh in September 1745, the Castle was garrisoned by government troops commanded by the eighty-five-year-old General Guest, and never surrendered to the Jacobites; from *The History of the Rebellion in the Year 1745* by John Home.

(The dramatist John Home, 1722–1808, fought on the Government side in the Jacobite rising of 1745 and wrote his account of the rising towards the end of his life.)

For some days after the battle of Preston, the communication between the castle and the town of Edinburgh continued open. The Highlanders kept guard at the Weigh House, and at some old buildings still nearer the castle; but allowed necessaries of every kind to pass, particularly for the use of the officers. By and by they began to be more strict; and on the 29th of September, orders were given to the guards to allow no person to pass or repass to the castle. That evening a letter was sent by General Guest to the Provost of Edinburgh, acquainting him, that unless a free communication was allowed between the castle and the town, the General would be obliged to make use of his cannon to dislodge the rebels who blockaded the castle. The Provost obtained a respite till next day, when six deputies were sent down to the Abbey. They presented to [*Prince*] Charles General Guest's letter, which was really intended for him. Charles gave an answer in writing expressing his surprise at the barbarity of the officer who threatened to bring distress upon the inhabitants of Edinburgh for not doing what was out of their power to do; and observing, that if compassion to the inhabitants of Edinburgh should make him withdraw his guards from their posts, General Guest might with equal reason require him to leave the city with his troops, and abandon all the advantages of his victory.

The citizens transmitted to General Guest the answer which Charles had made to his letter; and they obtained from the General a suspension of the threatened cannonade, till the return of an express which was sent to London. This delay was granted by the General, upon condition that the rebels, in the mean time, should attempt nothing against the castle. This condition, however, seems not to have been well understood; for on the 1st of October, the Highlanders having fired at some people whom they saw carrying provisions to the castle, the garrison next day fired both cannon and small arms at the houses that covered the Highland guard. Upon which Charles published a proclamation prohibiting all correspondence with the castle upon pain of death; and gave orders to stengthen the blockade by posting additional guards at several places. When General Guest was informed of this proclamation, and the orders given by Charles, he sent a message to the Magistrates of Edinburgh to acquaint them that he intended to demolish with his cannon those houses where the guards were posted, that prevented provisions being carried to the castle, but that care should be taken to do as little damage as possible to the inhabitants of the city. Accordingly about two o'clock on the 4th of October the cannonade began, and continued till the evening. As soon as it grew dark, the garrison made a sally, set fire to some of the houses that were next the castle, and made a trench between the castle and the upper end of the street, where they planted some field-pieces, and fired down the street with cartouch shot. Next day the cannonade continued, several of the rebels, and some of the inhabitants were killed or wounded. In the evening Charles published a proclamation recalling his orders, and allowing a communication between the town and the castle. This cannonade, or as it was called bombardment of Edinburgh, was grievously complained of. The generality of people conclude that the garrison of the castle was in want of provisions, and that the General found himself under the necessity of keeping the communication open in the manner he did. It was not so; the castle was well provided, and General Guest meant to engage the Highlanders in a siege; and prevent them from marching into England. With this view, in the beginning of the week after the battle of Preston, he wrote four or five letters addressed to the Duke of Newcastle, Secretary of State, acquainting his Grace, that there was but a very small stock of provisions in the castle of Edinburgh, that he would be obliged to surrender, if he was not relieved immediately; and he gave his advice, that the troops to relieve him should be sent by sea to Berwick or Newcastle, as the quickest conveyance. These letters were sent out from the castle, that they might fall into the hands of the rebels: but lest any of them should make its way through the Highlanders, and reach London, General Guest wrote a letter to the Duke of Newcastle, that contained an account of the real state of the garrison, and of the deception which he intended to practise on the rebels. This letter was sent to Captain Beaver of the Fox man of war, in the Road of Leith, by one Corsar, a writing master in Edinburgh, who desired Captain Beaver to send his long-boat to Berwick with the General's letter, and put it into the post-house there, that it might be safely conveyed to London. During this contest with General Guest, which lasted from the 29th of September to the 6th of October, very few people in Edinburgh or its neighbourhood joined the rebel army; and no man of quality but Lord Kilmarnock, and Arthur Elphinstone, who soon afterwards, by his brother's death, became Lord Balmerino.

[15] The rediscovery of the Scottish regalia in the Castle; from *The Prose works of Sir Walter Scott*, Volume VII.

(The regalia of Scotland – crown, sceptre and sword of state – had disappeared after the Act of Union of 1707, but were thought to have been deposited in a locked chest within the Crown Room of Edinburgh Castle. In 1817 Walter Scott was finally able to arrange for the location and formal opening of the chest.)

In the year 1794, the crown-room [*of the Castle*] was opened by special warrant under the royal sign manual to search for certain records which it was supposed might possibly have been deposited there. The dust of a century was upon the floor; the ashes of the last fire remained still in the chimney; no object was to be seen, excepting the great oak-chest so often mentioned, which the commissioners had no authority to open, their warrant having no relation to the regalia. The crown-room was secured with additional fastenings, and was again left to solitude and silence; the fate of the honours of Scotland remaining thus as uncertain as ever.

At length, in 1817, his royal highness, the Prince Regent, now King George the Fourth, influenced by that regard for the history and antiquities of his kingdom which well becomes his high station, and not uninterested, we may presume, in the development of the mystery which had so long hung over these insignia of royalty, was pleased to issue his warrant to the Scottish officers of state, and other public officers therein named, directing them to open the crown-room and search for the regalia, in order that their existence might be ascertained, and measures taken for their preservation. . . .

It was with feelings of no common anxiety that the commissioners, having read their warrant, proceeded to the crown-room; and having found all there in the state in which it had been left in 1794, commanded the King's Smith, who was in attendance, to force open the great chest, the keys of which had been sought for in vain. The general persuasion that the regalia had been secretly removed, weighed heavy upon the mind of all while the labour proceeded. The chest seemed to return a hollow and empty sound to the strokes of the hammer: and even those whose expectations had been most sanguine, felt at the moment the probability of disappointment, and could not but be sensible, that, should the result of the research confirm these forebodings, it would only serve to shew that a national affront and injury had been sustained, for which it might be difficult or rather impossible, to obtain any redress. The joy was therefore extreme, when, the ponderous lid of the chest being forced open, at the expense of some time and labour, the regalia were discovered lying at the bottom covered with linen cloths, exactly as they had been left in the year 1707, being about a hundred and ten years since they had been surrendered by William the ninth earl mareshal to the custody of the Earl of Glasgow, Treasurer-Deputy of Scotland. The relics were passed from hand to hand, and greeted with the affectionate reverence which emblems so venerable, restored to public view after the slumber of more than a hundred years, were so peculiarly calculated to excite. The discovery was instantly communicated to the public by the display of the royal standard from the castle, and was greeted by the shouts of the soldiers in garrison, and of a multitude of persons assembled on the Castle-hill; indeed the rejoicing was so general and sincere, as plainly to show, that, however altered in other respects, the people of Scotland had lost nothing of that national enthusiasm which formerly had displayed itself in grief for the loss of these emblematic honours, and now was expressed in joy for their recovery.

[16] The view from the Castle in 1878; from *Edinburgh, Picturesque Notes* by Robert Louis Stevenson.

The Old Town occupies a sloping ridge or tail of diluvial matter, protected, in some subsidence of the waters, by the Castle cliffs which fortify it to the west. On the one side of it and the other the new towns of the south and of the north occupy their lower, broader, and more gentle hill-tops. Thus, the quarter of the Castle overtops the whole city and keeps an open view to sea and land. It dominates for miles on every side; and people on the decks of ships, or ploughing in quiet country places over in Fife, can see the banner on the Castle battlements, and the smoke of the Old Town blowing abroad over the subjacent country. A city that is set upon a hill. It was, I suppose, from this distant aspect that she got her nickname of *Auld Reekie*. Perhaps it was given her by people who had never crossed her doors: day after day, from their various rustic Pisgahs, they had seen the pile of building on the hill-top, and the long plume of smoke over the plain; so it appeared to them; so it had appeared to their fathers tilling the same field; and as that was all they knew of the place, it could be all expressed in these two words.

Indeed, even on a nearer view, the Old Town is properly smoked; and though it is well washed with rain all the year round, it has a grim and sooty aspect among its younger suburbs. It grew, under the law that regulates the growth of walled cities in precarious situation, not in extent, but in height and density. Public buildings were forced, wherever there was room for them, into the midst of thoroughfares; thoroughfares were diminished into lanes; houses sprang up story after story, neighbour mounting upon neighbour's shoulder, as in some Black Hole of Calcutta, until the population slept fourteen or fifteen deep in a vertical direction. The tallest of these *lands*, as they are locally termed, have long since been burned out; but to this day it is not uncommon to see eight or ten windows at a flight; and the cliff of building which hangs imminent over Waverley Bridge would still put many natural precipices to shame. The cellars are already high above the gazer's head, planted on the steep hillside; as for the garret, all the furniture may be in the pawnshop, but it commands a famous prospect to the Highland hills. The poor man may roost up there in the centre of Edinburgh, and yet have a peep of the green country from his window; he shall see the quarters of the well-to-do fathoms underneath, with their broad squares and gardens; he shall have nothing overhead but a few spires, the stone top-gallants of the city; and perhaps the wind may reach him with a rustic pureness, and bring a smack of the sea, or of flowering lilacs in the spring.

High Street and Canongate, Mercat Cross, Tolbooth, Grassmarket

[17] The political conflicts of sixteenth-century Edinburgh resulted in a great deal of street brawling, of which the most serious occurred in 1520; from *Traditions of Edinburgh* by Robert Chambers.

(Robert Chambers, 1802–71, antiquary, essayist, editor and publisher, was among other things a great collector of Edinburgh traditions.)

It was in April 1520 that the Hamiltons (the party of the Earl of Arran), with Bethune, archbishop of Glasgow, called an assembly of the nobility in Edinburgh, in order to secure the government for the earl. The rival magnate, the Earl of Angus, soon saw danger to himself in the great crowds of the Hamilton party which flocked into town. Indeed warlike courses seem to have been determined on by that side. Angus sent his uncle, the bishop of Dunkeld, to caution them against any violence; and to offer that he should submit to the laws, if any offence were laid to his charge. The reverend prelate, proceeding to the place of assembly, which was in the archbishop's house, at the foot of Blackfriars' Wynd, found the Hamilton party obstinate. Thinking an archbishop could not or ought not to allow strife to take place if he could help it, he appealed to Bethune, who, however, had actually prepared for battle, by putting on armour under his rochet. 'Upon my conscience, my lord,' said Bethune, 'I know nothing of the matter,' at the same time striking his hand upon his breast, which caused the armour to return a rattling sound. Douglas's remark was simply, 'Your conscience clatters;' a happy pun for the occasion, clatter being a Scotch word signifying to tell tales. Gavin then returned to his lodging, and told his nephew that he must do his best to defend himself with arms. 'For me,' he said, 'I will go to my chamber and pray for

The High Street, Edinburgh, 1837; lithograph by S.D. Swarbreck – 'a fair, spacious, and capacious walk . . . the glory and beauty of this city'

you.' With our new light as to the locality of the bishop of Dunkeld's lodging, we now know that Angus and his uncle held their consultations on this occasion within fifty yards of the house in which the Hamiltons were assembled. The houses, in fact, nearly faced each other in the same narrow street.

Angus now put himself at the head of his followers, who, though not numerous, stood in a compact body in the High Street. They were, moreover, the favourites of the Edinburgh citizens, who handed spears from their windows to such as were not armed with that useful weapon. Presently the Hamiltons came thronging up from the Cowgate, through the narrow lanes, and entering the High Street in separate streams, armed with swords only, were at a great disadvantage. In a short time the Douglases had cleared the streets of them, killing many, and obliging Arran himself and his son to make their escape through the North Loch, mounted on a coal horse. Archbishop Bethune, with others, took refuge in the Blackfriars' Monastery, where he was seized behind the altar, and in danger of his life, when Gavin Douglas, learning his perilous situation, flew to save him, and with difficulty succeeded in his object. Here, too, local knowledge is important. The Blackfriars' Monastery stood where the High School latterly was, a spot not more than a hundred yards from the houses of both Bethune and Gavin Douglas. It would not necessarily require more than five minutes to apprise Douglas of Bethune's situation, and bring him to the rescue.

The popular name given to this street battle is characteristic – *Cleanse-the-Causeway.*

[18] The High Street and Canongate in 1598; from *An Itinerary written by Fynes Moryson, gent.*

From the Kings Pallace at the East, the city still riseth higher and higher towards the West, and consists especially of one broad and very faire street (which is the greatest part and sole ornament thereof), the rest of the side streetes and allies being of poore building and inhabited with very poore people, and this lengthe from the East to the West is about a mile, whereas the breadth of the City from the North to the South is narrow, and cannot be halfe a mile.

[19] The High Street and Canongate in 1636; from *The Diary of Sir William Brereton.*

Hence you may take a full view of the situation of the whole city, which is built upon a hill nothing oversteep, but sufficiently sloping and ascending to give a graceful ascent to the great street, which I do take to be an English mile long, and is the best paved street with bowther stones (which are very great ones) that I have seen: the channels are very conveniently contrived on both sides the streets, so as there is none in the middle; but it is the broadest, largest, and fairest pavement, and that entire, to go, ride, or drive upon.

Here they usually walk in the middle of the street, which is a fair, spacious, and capacious walk. This street is the glory and beauty of this city: it is the broadest street (except in the Low Countries, where there is a navigable channel in the middle of the street) and the longest street I have seen, which begins at the palace, the gate whereof enters straight into the suburbs, and is placed at the lower end of the same. The suburbs make an handsome street; and indeed the street, if the houses, which are very high, and substantially built of stone (some five, some six stories high), were not lined to the outside and faced with boards, it were the most stately and graceful street that ever I saw in my life; but this face of boards, which is towards the street, doth much blemish it, and derogate from glory and beauty; as also the want of fair glass windows, whereof few or none are to be discerned towards the street, which is the more complete, because it is as straight as may be. This lining with boards (wherein are round holes shaped to the proportion of men's heads), and this encroachment into the street about two yards, is a mighty disgrace unto it, for the walls (which were the outside) are stone; so, as if this outside facing of boards were removed, and the houses built uniform all of the same height, it were the most complete street in Christendom.

[20] The execution of James Graham, fifth Earl and first Marquis of Montrose, at the Mercat Cross in 1560; from *Memoirs of the Marquis of Montrose* by Mark Napier.

(The Marquis of Montrose had raised a largely Highland army to fight for Charles I in the Civil War, but after some spectacular victories he was defeated at the battle of Philiphaugh in 1645. He escaped, wandered around Scotland, was finally routed with his relatively few supporters at Carbisdale in 1650, and was executed on 21 May.

Mark Napier (1776–1847) was a Scottish historical biographer who published important biographies, based on original sources, of a number of significant figures in Scottish history.)

Relation from Edinburgh concerning the hanging of Montrose, May 21st, 1650.

'What with the early going away of the post, and what with the hubub we are in, – *Montrose being now on the scaffold*, – I must cut short: –

'Saturday, he was brought into the town, sitting tied with a rope upon a high chair, upon a cart; the hangman having before taken off his hat, and riding before him with his bonnet on. Several have been with him. He saith for personal offences he hath deserved all this; but justifies his cause. He caused a new suit to be made for himself; and came yesterday into the Parliament House with a scarlet rochet, and suit of pure cloth all laid with rich lace, a beaver and rich hat-band, and scarlet silk stockings. The Chancellor made a large speech to him; discovering how much formerly he was for the Covenant, and how he hath since broke it. He [Montrose] desired to know whether he might be free to answer? And being admitted he told them his cause was good; and that he had not only a *commission* but *particular orders* for what he had done, from his Majesty, which he was engaged to be a Servant to: and they also had professed to comply: and upon that account, however they dealt with him, yet he would own them to be a true Parliament. And he further told them, that, if they would take away his life, *the world knew he regarded it not*; that it was a debt that must once be paid; and that he was willing, and did much rejoice, that he must go the same way his master did; and it was the joy of his heart, not only to do but to suffer for him.

'His sentence was, to be hanged upon a gallows thirty feet high, three hours, at Edinburgh Cross; to have his head strucken off, and hanged upon Edinburgh Tolbooth, and his arms and legs to be hanged up in other public towns in the kingdom, as Glasgow, &c., and his body to be buried at the common burying-place, in case excommunication from the Kirk was taken off; or else to be buried where those are buried that were hanged.

'All the time, while the sentence was given, and also when he was executed, he seemed no way to be altered, or his spirit moved; but his speech was *full of composure*, and his carriage as sweet as ever I saw a man in all my days. When they bid him kneel, he told them he would; he was willing to observe any posture that might manifest his obedience, especially to them who were so near conjunction with his master. It is absolutely believed that he hath overcome more men by his death, in Scotland, than he would have done if he had lived. For I never saw a more sweeter carriage in a man in all my life.

'I should write more largely if I had time; *but he is just now a turning off from the ladder*: but his countenance changes not. . . .'

[21] The High Street in the mid-seventeenth century; from *Epistolae Ho-Elianae: Familiar Letters Domestic and Forren* by James Howell.

(James Howell, English author, traveller and diplomat, visited Edinburgh in 1639. At this time Scottish Presbyterians were enraged by Charles I's attempt to force episcopacy on them.)

This town of Edinburgh is one of the fairest streets that ever I saw (excepting that of Palermo in Sicily), it is about a mile long, coming sloping down from the Castle . . . to Holyroodhouse, now the royal palace; and these two begin and terminate the town. I am come hither in a very convenient time, for here is a national assembly, and a parliament, my Lord Traquair being his Majesty's Commissioner. The bishops are all gone to wreck, and they have had but a sorry funeral: the very name is grown so contemptible that a black dog, if he hath any white marks about him, is called Bishop. Our Lord of Canterbury is grown here so odious, that they call him commonly in the pulpit, the Priest of Baal, and the son of Belial.

[22] Strange animals in the Canongate, in the 1650s; from *A Diary of Public Transactions and Other Occurrences Chiefly in Scotland from 1650 to 1667* by John Nicoll.

(John Nicoll, c.1590–c.1667, was born in Glasgow but spent most of his life in Edinburgh, where he was a Writer to the Signet and a notary public.)

At this tyme, thair was brocht to this natioun ane heigh great beast, callit ane Drommodrary, quhilk being keipit clos in the Cannongait, nane hade a sight of it without thrie pence the persone, quhilk producit much gayne to the keipar. ... Thair wes brocht in with it any lytill baboun, faced lyke unto a naip.

[23] Charles II is proclaimed King at the Mercat Cross, May 1660; from *A Diary of Public Transactions* ... by John Nicoll.

This Proclamation ... was ... proclaimed at the Mercat Cross of Edinburgh, upone Monday thaireftir, being the 14 of the same moneth, with all solempniteis requisite, by ringing of bellis, setting out of bailfyres, sounding of trumpetis, roring of cannounes, touking of drumes, dancing about the fyres, and using all uther takins of joy for the advancement and preference of thair native King to his crown and native inheritance. Quhairat also, thair wes much wyne spent, the spoutes of the croce ryning and venting out abundance of wyne, placed thair for that end; and the magistrates and counsell of the toun being present, drinking the Kinges helth, and breking numberis of glasses.

The Canongate, looking west; by Thomas Shepherd from *Modern Athens . . .,* 1829

[24] The execution of Argyll at the Mercat Cross, 1685; from *The History of the Sufferings of the Church of Scotland* by the Rev. Robert Wodrow.

(Archibald Campbell, 9th Earl of Argyll, tried and condemned to death for treason in 1681, escaped to Holland from Edinburgh Castle, disguised as a page. He returned to England in 1685 to take part in the ill-fated Monmouth insurrection against James VII and II, and was executed in 1685 in terms of the original sentence of 1681.

Robert Wodrow, 1679–1734, was University Librarian at

Glasgow from 1697 to 1701 and later became minister of
Eastwood. He collected material on the history of the Covenanters, on which he left numerous manuscript collections as well as
his published work.)

June 28th, being the sabbath before his death, the earl spent it in
the most spiritual and heavenly manner could be; and indeed to
him it was a prelude of the everlasting sabbatism he was just
entering upon. His sister, the lady Lothian, came to take her
leave of him, and was very much affected; which the earl
perceiving, said to her, 'I am now loosed from you, and all earthly
satisfactions, and long to be with Christ, which is far better. It
seemeth, the Lord thought not me fit to be an instrument in his
work, but I die in the faith of it, that it will advance, and that the
Lord will appear. ...' His father, I may say, was our first and
proto-martyr, and after, his son, and some few others, who, as we
shall hear, suffered upon the same account. We have not many
more sufferers to death till the deliverance come. As the noble
marquis his father went first, and his blood opened, as it were, the
floodgates to a great stream we have seen running, so the son
almost closes up this river of blood, shed for our religion and holy
reformation. His expressions are heroically Christian, with
relation to his family and posterity, and some way prophetical;
they have indeed been wonderfully seen to and provided for,
and, even as to their outward estate and grandeur, advanced to
greater honour and riches than the earl or marquis had . . .

    The earl was beheaded Tuesday, June 30th. In the morning,
he had, in the greatest throng of necessary avocations, much
calmness and serenity of soul, yea much joy and peace, in
believing. We have observed the same in relation to his father.
To one standing by him the earl said, 'I have more joy and
comfort this day, than the day after I escaped out of the castle;'
and I nothing doubt that it continued with him, until he entered
into the joy of his Lord.

[25] Anti-Union riots in the High Street, 1706; from *The Letters of Daniel Defoe.*

(The novelist and pamphleteer Daniel Defoe was sent to Edinburgh by Robert Harley, Secretary of State and Lord Treasurer under Queen Anne, to propagandize for the Union and report to Harley on developments.)

We have had Two Mobbs since my last and Expect a Third and of these the Following is a short account.

The first was in the Assembly or Commission of Assembly where Very strange things were Talk'd of and in a strange Manner and I Confess Such as has put me Much Out of Love with Ecclesiastic Parliamts. The Power, Anglice Tyranny, of the Church was here Describd to the life and Jure Divino Insisted upon In prejudice to Civill Authourity – but this was by some Tumultuous spirits who are Over ruld by men of More Moderation, and as an Assembly they act with more wisdom and Honesty than they do in Their private Capascities in which I Confess they Contribute too Much to the Generall Aversion which here is to the Union, at the Same Time they Acknowlege they are Unsafe and Uneasy in Their present Establishment – I work Incessantly with them. They go from me seemingly Satisfyed and pretend to be Informd but are the Same Men when they Come Among Their parties – I hope what I say to you Sir shall Not prejudice them; in Generall They are the Wisest weak men, The Falsest honest men, and the steadyest Unsettled people Ever I met with. They Mean well but are blinded in their politicks and Obstinate in Opinion.

But we had the last Two Nights a worse Mob than this and that was in the street, and Certainly a scots Rabble is the worst of its kind.

The first night they Onely Threatned hard and follow'd their Patron D. Hamilton's Chair with Huzzas from the Parliament house quite Thro' the City – They Came up again Hallowing in the Dark, Threw some stones at the Guard, broke a few windows and the like, and so it Ended.

I was warn'd that night that I should Take Care of my Self and not Appear in the street which Indeed for the last five dayes I have done Very Little haveing been Confin'd by a Violent Cold. However, I went up the street in a Friends Coach in the Evening and some of the Mob Not then Gott together were heard to say when I went into a house, There was One of the English Dogs &c.

I Casually stayd at the house I went then to Till Dark and Thinking to Return to my Lodging, found the wholl City in a Most Dreadfull Uproar and the high street Full of the Rabble.

Duke Hamilton Came from the House in his Chair as Usuall and Instead of Goeing Down the City to his Lodgings Went up the High Street *as was said* to Visit the D of Athol.

This whether Design'd by the D. as Most think or No, but if not was Exactly Calculated to begin the Tumult – For the Mob in a Vast Crow'd attending him thither waited at the Door – and as those people did not Come there to be Idle, The Duke Could have Done Nothing more Directly to point Out their bussiness, The Late Ld Provost Sir Pat. Johnston liveing just upon the spot.

The Mob had Threatned him before and I had been Told he had Such Notice of it That he Remov'd himself; Others Say he was in his Lodgings with 11 or 12 Gentlemen besides Servants Resolved to Defend himself; but be That as it will.

The Mob Came up staires to his Door and fell to work with sledges to break it Open, but it seems Could not. His Lady in the Fright with Two Candles in her hand that she might be known, Opens the Windows and Cries Out for God Sake to Call the Guard.

An Honest Townsman, an Apothecary, that Saw the Distress the Family was In went Down to the Guard which is kept in the Middle of the street, and Found the Officers Very Indifferent in the Matter, whether as to the Cause or is Rather Judg'd Thro' Reall fear of the Rabble, but Applying himself to One Capt Richardson, a brave Resolute Officer, he told him he Could Not go from the Guard without the Ld Provosts Ordr but if he would Obtain that ordr he would go up – In short the Ordr was Obtain'd and the Capt went with a Party of the Guard and made his way Thro' the Rable to Sir Pat. Johnston's stair Case – The Generallity of them fled, some were knock't Down and the stair

Case Clear'd, and Three or four Taken in the Very assaulting the Door.

Yet they fled Not far but Hallowing and Throwing stones and sticks at the souldiers Severall of Them are Very Much bruised and the brave Capt I am Told keeps his bed.

However, he brought Down his prisoners and the Toll booth being at hand Hurryed them in and made his Retreat to the Guard.

In This posture Things stood about 8 to 9 a Clock and the street seeming passable I Sallyed Out and Got to my Lodging.

I had not been Long There but I heard a Great Noise and looking Out Saw a Terrible Multitude Come up the High street with A Drum at the head of Them shouting and swearing and Cryeing Out all scotland would stand together, No Union, No Union, English Dogs, and the like.

[26] The High Street and Canongate in the 1720s; from *Tour thro' the Whole Island of Britain* by Daniel Defoe.

At the Extremity of the East-end of the City stands the Palace of *Holy-rood house*; leaving which, a little to the Left, you come through a populous Suburb to the entrance, called the *Water-port*. From hence, turning West, the Street goes on, in a strait Line, through the whole City, to the Castle. It is above a Mile in Length; and is, perhaps, the largest, longest, and finest Street, for Buildings, and Number of Inhabitants, in the World.

[27] The escape of one smuggler from the Tolbooth Church, and the execution of another in the Grassmarket; from *The Autobiography of Dr Alexander Carlyle of Inveresk 1722–1805*.

(Alexander Carlyle, 1722–1805, known as 'Jupiter' Carlyle, was minister of Inveresk, a leader of the Moderate party in the Church of Scotland, and a prominent member of the Edinburgh literati.)

I was witness to a very extraordinary scene that happened in the month of February or March 1736, which was the escape of Robertson, a condemned criminal, from the Tolbooth Church in Edinburgh. In those days it was usual to bring the criminals who were condemned to death into that church, to attend public worship every Sunday after their condemnation, when the clergyman made some part of his discourse and prayers to suit their situation; which, among other circumstances of solemnity which then attended the state of condemned criminals, had no small effect on the public mind. Robertson and Wilson were smugglers, and had been condemned for robbing a custom-house, where some of their goods had been deposited; a crime which at that time did not seem, in the opinion of the common people, to deserve so severe a punishment. I was carried by an acquaintance to church to see the prisoners on the Sunday before the day of execution. We went early into the church on purpose to see them come in, and were seated in a pew before the galley in front of the pulpit. Soon after we went into the church by the door from the Parliament Close, the criminals were brought in by the door next the Tolbooth, and placed in a long pew, not far from the pulpit. Four soldiers came in with them, and placed Robertson at the head of the pew, and Wilson below him, two themselves sitting below Wilson, and two in a pew behind him.

The bells were ringing and the doors were open, while the people were coming into the church. Robertson watched his opportunity, and, suddenly springing up, got over the pew into the passage that led in to the door in the Parliament Close, and no person offering to lay hands on him, made his escape in a moment – so much the more easily, perhaps, as everybody's attention was drawn to Wilson, who was a stronger man, and who, attempting to follow Robertson, was seized by the soldiers, and struggled so long with them that the two who at last followed Robertson were too late. It was reported that he had maintained his struggle that he might let his companion have time. That might be his second thought, but his first certainly was to escape himself, for I saw him set his foot on the seat to leap over, when the soldiers pulled him back. Wilson was immediately carried out to the Tolbooth, and Robertson, getting uninterrupted through the Parliament Square, down the back stairs, into the Cowgate, was heard of no more till he arrived in Holland. This was an interesting scene, and by filling the public mind with compassion for the unhappy person who did not escape, and who was the better character of the two, had probably some influence in producing what followed: for when the sentence against Wilson came to be executed a few weeks thereafter, a very strong opinion prevailed that there was a plot to force the Town Guard, whose duty it is to attend executions under the order of a civil magistrate.

There was a Captain Porteous, who by his good behaviour in the army had obtained a subaltern's commission, and had afterwards, when on half-pay, been preferred to the command of the City Guard. This man, by his skill in manly exercises, particularly the golf, and by gentlemanly behaviour, was admitted into the company of his superiors, which elated his mind, and added insolence to his native roughness, so that he was much hated and feared by the mob of Edinburgh. When the day of execution came, the rumour of a deforcement at the gallows prevailed strongly; and the Provost and Magistrates (both in their own minds very strong) thought it a good measure to apply for three or four companies of a marching regiment that lay in the Canongate, to be drawn up in the Lawnmarket, a street leading from the Tolbooth to the Grassmarket, the place of execution, in order to overawe the mob by their being at hand. Porteous, who, it is said, had his natural courage increased to rage by any suspicion that he and his Guard could not execute the law, and being heated likewise with wine – for he had dined, as the custom then was, between one and two – became perfectly furious when he passed by the three companies drawn up in the street as he marched along with his prisoner.

Mr Baillie had taken windows in a house on the north side of the Grassmarket, for his pupils and me, in the second floor, about seventy or eighty yards westward of the place of execution, where we went in due time to see the show; to which I had no small aversion having seen one at Dumfries, the execution of Jock Johnstone, which shocked me very much. When we arrived at the house, some people who were looking from the windows were displaced, and went to a window in the common stair, about two feet below the level of ours. The street is long and wide, and there was a very great crowd assembled. The execution went on with the usual forms, and Wilson behaved in a manner very becoming his situation. There was not the least appearance of an attempt to rescue; but soon after the executioner had done his duty, there was an attack made upon him, as usual on such occasions, by the boys and blackguards throwing stones and dirt in testimony of their abhorrence of the hangman. But there was no attempt to break through the guard and cut down the prisoner. It was generally said that there was very little, if any, more violence than had usually happened on such occasions. Porteous, however, inflamed with wine and jealousy, thought proper to order his Guard to fire, their muskets being loaded with slugs; and when the soldiers showed reluctance, I saw him turn to them with threatening gesture and an inflamed countenance. They obeyed, and fired; but wishing to do as little harm as possible, many of them elevated their pieces, the effect of which was that some people were wounded in the windows; and one unfortunate lad, whom we had displaced, was killed in the stair window by a slug entering his head. His name was Henry Black, a journeyman tailor, whose bride was the daughter of the house we were in. She fainted away when he was brought into the house speechless, where he only lived till nine or ten o'clock. We had seen many people, women and men, fall on the street, and at first thought it was only through fear, and by their crowding on one another to escape. But when the crowd dispersed, we saw them lying dead or wounded, and had no longer any doubt of what had happened. The numbers were said to be eight or nine killed, and double the number wounded; but this was never exactly known.

This unprovoked slaughter irritated the common people to the last; and the state of grief and rage into which their minds were thrown, was visible in the high commotion that appeared in the multitude.

The Castle from the Grassmarket; pen-and-wash drawing by W. Geikie *c.*1820

[28] The lynching of Captain Porteous in the Grassmarket; from *The Heart of Midlothian* by Walter Scott.

(Captain Porteous was tried and condemned to death for his part in the incident described above, but he was subsequently reprieved, to the fury of the Edinburgh mob who stormed the Tolbooth prison, where Porteous was confined while awaiting execution, and removed him by force as he tried to escape up a chimney.)

They had suffered the unfortunate Porteous to put on his night-gown and slippers, as he had thrown off his coat and shoes, in order to facilitate his attempted escape up the chimney. In this garb he was now mounted on the hands of two of the rioters, clasped together, so as to form what is called in Scotland, 'The King's Cushion'. Butler was placed close to his side, and repeatedly urged to perform a duty always the most painful which can be imposed on a clergyman deserving of the name, and now rendered more so by the peculiar and horrid circum-stances of the criminal's case. Porteous at first uttered some supplications for mercy, but when he found that there was no chance that these would be attended to, his military education, and the natural stubbornness of his disposition, combined to support his spirits.

'Are you prepared for this dreadful end?' said Butler in a faltering voice. 'O turn to Him, in whose eyes time and space have no existence, and to whom a few minutes are as a lifetime, and a lifetime as a minute.'

'I believe I know what you would say,' answered Porteous sullenly. 'I was bred a soldier; if they will murder me without time, let my sins as well as my blood lie at their door.'

'Who was it,' said the stern voice of Wildfire, 'that said to Wilson at this very spot, when he could not pray, owing to the galling agony of his fetters, that his pains would soon be over? – I say to you take your own tale home; and if you cannot profit by the good man's lessons, blame not them that are still more merciful to you than you were to others.'

The procession now moved forward with a slow and deter-mined pace. It was enlightened by many blazing links and torches; for the actors of this work were so far from affecting any secrecy on the occasion, that they seemed even to court observation. Their principal leaders kept close to the person of the prisoner, whose pallid yet stubborn features were seen distinctly by the torchlight, as his person was raised considerably above the concourse which thronged around him. Those who bore swords, muskets, and battle-axes, marched on each side, as if forming a regular guard to the procession. The windows, as they went along, were filled with the inhabitants, whose slumbers had been broken by this unusual disturbance. Some of the spectators muttered accents of encouragement; but in general they were so much appalled by a sight so strange and audacious, that they looked on with a sort of stupefied astonishment. No one offered, by act or word, the slightest interruption.

The rioters, on their part, continued to act with the same air of deliberate confidence and security which had marked all their proceedings. When the object of their resentment dropped one of his slippers, they stopped, sought for it, and replaced it upon his foot with great deliberation. As they descended the Bow towards the fatal spot [*the Grassmarket*] where they designed to complete their purpose, it was suggested that there should be a rope kept in readiness. For this purpose the booth of a man who dealt in cordage was forced open, a coil of rope fit for their purpose was selected to serve as a halter, and the dealer next morning found that a guinea had been left on his counter in exchange; so anxious were the perpetrators of this daring action to show that they meditated not the slightest wrong or infraction of law, excepting so far as Porteous was himself concerned.

Leading, or carrying, along with them, in this determined and regular manner, the object of their vengeance, they at length reached the place of common execution, the scene of his crime, and destined spot of his sufferings. Several of the rioters (if they should not rather be described as conspirators) endeavoured to remove the stone which filled up the socket in which the end of the fatal tree was sunk when it was erected for its fatal purpose; others sought for the means of constructing a temporary gibbet, the place in which the gallows itself was deposited being reported too secure to be forced, without much loss of time. Butler endeavoured to avail himself of the delay afforded by these circumstances, to turn the people from their desperate design. 'For God's sake,' he exclaimed, 'remember it is the image of your Creator which you are about to deface in the person of this unfortunate man! Wretched as he is, and wicked as he may be, he has a share in every promise of Scripture, and you cannot destroy him in impenitence without blotting his name from the Book of Life – Do not destroy soul and body; give time for preparation.'

'What time had they,' returned a stern voice, 'whom he

murdered on this very spot? – The laws both of God and man call for his death.'

'But what, my friends,' insisted Butler, with a generous disregard to his own safety – 'what hath constituted you his judges?'

'We are not his judges,' replied the same person; 'he has been already judged and condemned by lawful authority. We are those whom Heaven, and our righteous anger, have stirred up to execute judgement, when a corrupt government would have protected a murderer.'

'I am none,' said the unfortunate Porteous; 'that which you charge upon me fell out in self-defence, in the lawful exercise of my duty.'

'Away with him – away with him!' was the general cry. 'Why do you trifle away time in making a gallows? – that dyester's pole is good enough for the homicide.'

The unhappy man was forced to his fate with remorseless rapidity. Butler, separated from him by the press, escaped the last horrors of his struggles. Unnoticed by those who had hitherto detained him as a prisoner, he fled from the fatal spot, without much caring in what direction his course lay. A loud shout proclaimed the stern delight with which the agents of this deed regarded its completion. Butler, then, at the opening into the low street called the Cowgate, cast back a terrified glance, and, by the red and dusky light of the torches, he could discern a figure wavering and struggling as it hung suspended above the heads of the multitude, and could even observe men striking at it with their Lochaber-axes and partisans. The sight was of a nature to double his horror, and to add wings to his flight.

[29] Buildings in the High Street in 1769; from *A Tour in Scotland MDCCLXIX* by Thomas Pennant.

(Thomas Pennant was a traveller and naturalist of Queen's College, Oxford.)

A city that possesses a boldness and grandeur of situation beyond any that I have ever seen. It is built on the edges and sides of a vast sloping rock, of a great and precipitous height at the upper extremity, and the sides declining very quick and steep into the plain. The view of the houses at a distance strikes the traveller with wonder; their own loftiness, improved by their almost aerial situation, gives them a look of magnificence not to be found in any other part of *Great Britain*. All these conspicuous buildings form the upper part of the great street, are of stone, and make a handsome appearance: they are generally six or seven stories high in front; but, by reason of the declivity of the hill, much higher backward; one in particular, called *Babel*, has about twelve or thirteen stories. Every house has a common staircase, and every story is the habitation of a separate family.

[30] The High Street market in 1774; from *Letters from Edinburgh; Written in the Years 1774 and 1775* by Captain Edward Topham.

(Edward Topham, English journalist, playwright and Captain in the Life Guards, travelled both abroad and in Scotland.)

You have seen the famous street at Lisle, La Rue royale, leading to the port of Tournay, which is said to be the finest in Europe; but which I can assure you is not to be compared either in length or breadth to the High Street at Edinburgh: and would they be at the expence of removing some buildings which obstruct the view, by being placed in the middle of the street, nothing could be conceived more magnificent. Not content, however, with this, they suffer a weekly market to be held, in which stalls are erected nearly the whole length of it, and make a confusion almost impossible to be conceived. All sorts of iron and copper ware are exposed to sale; here likewise the herb market is held, and the herb women, who are in no country either the most peaceable or the most cleanly beings upon earth, throw about the roots, stalks, &c of the bad vegetables, to the great nusance of the passengers.

The style of building here is much like the French: the houses, however, in general are higher, as some rise to twelve, and one in particular to thirteen stories in height. But to the front of the street nine or ten stories is the common run; it is the back part of the edifice which, by being built on the slope of an hill, sinks to that amazing depth, so as to form the above number. This mode of dwelling, tho' very proper for the turbulent times to which it was adapted, has now lost its convenience: as they no longer stand in need of the defence from the castle, they no more find the benefit of being crowded together so near it. The common staircase which leads to the apartments of the different inhabitants, must always be dirty, and is in general very dark and narrow. It has this advantage, however, that as they are all of stone, they have little to apprehend from fire, which, in the opinion of some, would more than compensate for every other disadvantage. In general, however, the highest and lowest tenements are possessed by the artificers, while the gentry and better sort of people dwell in fifth and sixth stories . . .

[31] The High Street in 1805; from *The Beauties of Scotland* by Robert Forsyth.

Many specimens of buildings of considerable antiquity remain in the High Street of Edinburgh and adjoining to it. In 1698 a statute of the Scottish Parliament prohibited any house to be built higher than five stories from the ground. All those houses, therefore, which exceed that height, must have been built previous to the statute. The law only applies to such parts of a house as front a public street or lane. Hence it frequently happens, in consequence of the singular inequality of the ground, that while the front of a house rises to no more than the statutory height, its back part is eight or ten, or even twelve stories high. All these stories are inhabited by separate families; and in the course of time it sometimes happens that the back of one of these houses comes to front a newly opened street. In which case, however, if it fall into decay, it is generally understood that it cannot be rebuilt of the same height. The habit which the inhabitants of Edinburgh have acquired of living above each other in separate stories, with a common stair from which they all enter, together with the high price which a very small extent of ground brings when sold, induces proprietors, when rebuilding their houses, still to rear them as high as the law will permit, that they may derive the highest possible profit from their property.

The High Street of Edinburgh receives from the inhabitants different appellations to distinguish different parts of it. Near the Castle it is termed the *Castle-hill*: somewhat lower down, it is called the *Lawn-market*, from a branch of trade formerly carried on there: at the lower end of the Lawn-market where stands the ancient Episcopal Cathedral, or Church of St Giles, the street for considerable distance is called, by way of distinction, the *High Street*; this being the most frequented and public part of it. Farther down the hill, at a place where the city wall anciently crossed it, the High Street takes the appellation of the *Canongate*, which continues downwards to the Palace.

[32] The great fire of 1824; from *Edinburgh in the Nineteenth Century, being a diary of the chief events which have occurred in the city from 1800 AD to 1900 AD*, edited by W.M. Gilbert.

The most disastrous fire recorded in the history of the city broke out on Monday night, the 15th November, about ten o'clock, in a large seven-story house at the head of the Old Assembly Close, and, with the exception of one tenement left standing opposite the Cross, the whole buildings on the south side of the High Street, from the head of the Old Assembly Close round to the Exchequer buildings in Parliament Square, were destroyed, together with much of the property running backward to the Cowgate. The fire burned fiercely the whole night, the old houses, full of dry wooden panelling, affording abundant food for the flames, which only began to abate about nine o'clock on the following morning. While the conflagration was raging great showers of sparks and burning embers fell upon the street and adjoining buildings, some of which were fired in that way. A tenement, in which the *Courant* newspaper office was situated, was totally destroyed. To the west of this the conflagration was arrested by the fact that the tenement overtopped the others by a story. On Tuesday fore-noon, when all danger seemed to be past, the steeple of the Tron Church was discovered to be on fire. Some burning embers had been carried to the balustrade, and had been fanned into a flame by the wind, which, though it had been calm all night, was now blowing a gale. The steeple was of wood cased in lead, and blazed furiously. The firemen had to fly for their lives, for the molten lead poured down the sides of the structure, and rendered it impossible to approach it with safety. The heat was so great that a large bell weighing two tons, which had been hung in 1673, was fused. The steeple burned for three-quarters of an hour, and then fell with a crash. By great exertions the firemen managed to save the church. The same evening, fire broke out again in a tenement on the south side of Parliament Square, with its back overlooking the Cowgate. It was an immense pile, eleven stories in height, and it burned with irresistible fury. The flames spread to the east side of the Square, and all that was left standing by the June fire was then involved in the general destruction. The value of the property destroyed by these conflagrations was estimated at £200,000, nearly four hundred families were rendered for the time homeless, and eight individuals were either killed on the spot by the falling of ruins or died in consequence of their hurts. Along the front of the High Street there were destroyed four lands of six stories each; towards Cowgate by Con's Close, two wooden lands; in the Old Assembly Close, four lands of six or seven stories; six smaller tenements in Borthwick's Close; and four lands of from six to nine stories in the Old Fishmarket Close. Along the front of Parliament Square four double lands, of from seven to eleven stories in height, were destroyed. The dangerous walls left standing of the burned houses were brought down on the following Saturday by means of a chain cable and apparatus worked by a body of H.M seamen, and partly by mining with gunpowder.

The West Bow

[33] Character of the West Bow; from *Traditions of Edinburgh* by Robert Chambers.

In a central part of Old Edinburgh – the very little Britain of our city ⌐ is a curious, angular, whimsical-looking street, of great steepness and narrowness, called the West Bow. Serving as a connexion between the Grassmarket and Lawnmarket, between the Low and the High Town, it is of considerable fame in our city annals as a passage for the entry of sovereings, and the scene of the quaint ceremonials used on those occasions. In more modern times, it has been chiefly notable in the recollections of country people as a nest of the peculiarly noisy tradesmen, the white-iron smiths, which causes Robert Fergusson to mark, as one of the features of Edinburgh deserted for a holiday –

'The tinkler billies o' the Bow
Are now less eident clinkin.'

Another remarkable circumstance connected with the street in the popular mind, is its having been the residence of the famed wizard Major Weir. All of these particulars serve to make it a noteworthy sort of place, and the impression is much favoured by its actual appearance. A perfect Z in figure, composed of tall antique houses, with numerous dovecot-like gables projecting over the footway, full of old inscriptions and sculpturings, presenting at every few steps some darksome lateral profundity, into which the imagination wanders without hindrance or exhaustion, it seems eminently a place of old grandmothers' tales, and sure at all times to maintain a ghost or two in its community.

[34] The story of Major Weir, 1670; from *Traditions of Edinburgh* by Robert Chambers.

It must have been a sad scandal to this peculiar community when Major Weir, one of their number, was found to have been so wretched an example of human infirmity. The house occupied by this man still exists, though in an altered shape, in a little court accessible by a narrow passage near the first angle of the street. His history is obscurely reported; but it appears that he was of a good family in Lanarkshire, and had been one of the ten thousand men sent by the Scottish Covenanting Estates in 1641 to assist in suppressing the Irish Papists. Having afterwards risen to the rank of major in the Town-Guard of Edinburgh, he became distinguished for a life of peculiar sanctity, even in an age when that was the prevailing tone of the public mind. According to a contemporary account, 'His garb was still a cloak, and somewhat dark, and he never went without his staff. He was a tall black man, and ordinarily looked down to the ground; *a grim countenance, and a big nose.* At length he became so notoriously regarded among the Presbyterian strict sect, that if four met together, be sure Major Weir was one. At private meetings he prayed to admiration, which made many of that stamp court his converse. He never married, but lived in a private lodging with his sister Grizel Weir. Many resorted to his house, to join with him, and hear him pray; but it was observed that he could not officiate in any holy duty without the black staff, or rod, in his hand, and leaning upon it, which made those who heard him pray admire his flood in prayer, his ready extemporary expression, his heavenly gesture; so that he was thought more angel than man, and was termed by some of the holy sisters ordinarily *Angelical Thomas.*' Plebeian imaginations have since fructified regarding the staff, and crones will still seriously tell how it could run a message to a shop for any article which its proprietor wanted; how it could answer the door when any one called upon its master; and that it used to be often seen running before him, in the capacity of a link-boy, as he walked down the Lawnmarket.

After a life characterised externally by all the graces of devotion, but polluted in secret by crimes of the most revolting nature, and which little needed the addition of wizardry to excite the horror of living men, Major Weir fell into a severe sickness, which affected his mind so much, that he made open and voluntary confession of all his wickedness. The tale was at first so incredible, that the provost, Sir Andrew Ramsay, refused for some time to take him into custody. At length himself, his sister (partner of one of his crimes), and his staff, were secured by the magistrates, together with certain sums of money, which were found wrapped up in rags in different parts of the house. One of these pieces of rag being thrown into the fire by a bailie who had taken the whole in charge, flew up the chimney, and made an explosion like a cannon. While the wretched man lay in prison, he made no scruple to disclose the particulars of his guilt, but refused to address himself to the Almighty for pardon. To every request that he would pray, he answered in screams, 'Torment me no more – I am tormented enough already!' Even the offer of a Presbyterian clergyman, instead of an established Episcopal minister of the city, had no effect upon him. He was tried April 9, 1670, and being found guilty, was sentenced to be strangled and burnt between Edinburgh and Leith. His sister, who was tried at the same time, was sentenced to be hanged in the Grassmarket. The execution of the profligate major took place, April 14, at the place indicated by the judge. When the rope was about his neck, to prepare him for the fire, he was bid to say, 'Lord, be merciful to me!' but he answered, as before, 'Let me alone – I will not – I have lived as a beast, and I must die as a beast!' After he had dropped lifeless in the flames, his stick was also cast into the fire; and 'whatever incantation was in it,' says the contemporary writer already quoted, 'the persons present own that it gave rare turnings, and was long a-burning, as also himself.'

Holyrood Abbey and
the Palace of Holyroodhouse

[35] The founding of Holyrood Abbey by David I in 1128; from *The Description of Scotland, written at first by Hector Boethius in Latin and afterwards translated into the Scottish Speech by John Bellenden, Archdeacon of Murray, and now finallie in English by W.H.*

(W.H. was William Harrison, 1534 to 1593, topographer and chronologist.)

He [*David I*] was admonished (as the report goeth) in his sleepe, that he should build an abbeie for a religious order to live in together. Whereupon he sent for workmen into *France* and *Flanders*, and set them in hand to build this abbeie of canons regular, as he was admonished, dedicating it in the honor of a crosse (whereunto he bare speciall devotion) for that verie strangelie it slipped into his hands (on a time) as he was pursuing and following of a hart in the chase.

[36] The trial of John Knox before the Privy Council at the Palace of Holyroodhouse, 1563; from *The History of the Reformation in Scotland* by John Knox.

Within four days the said John Knox was called before Queen Mary and the Privy Council (at Holyrood), between six and seven hours at night. The season of the year was the middle of December. The bruit rising in the town, that John Knox was sent for by the Queen, the brethren of the Kirk followed in such numbers, that the Inner Close was full, and all the stairs, even to the chamber door, where the Queen and Council sat. They had been reasoning among themselves before, but had not fully satisfied the mind of the Secretary. So the Queen had retired to her cabinet, and the Lords were talking each one with the other, as occasion served. But upon the entry of John Knox, they were commanded to take their places, and so they did, sitting as Councillors one over against another. . . .

Things thus put in order, the Queen came forth, and with no little worldly pomp, was placed in the chair, having two faithful supports, Sir John Maxwell of Terregles, Master of Maxwell upon the one tor (*arm*), and Secretary Lethington on the other tor of the chair, whereupon they waited diligently all the time of that accusation, sometimes the one occupying her ear, sometimes the other. Her pomp lacked one principal point, to wit WOMANLY GRAVITY: for when she saw John Knox standing at the other end of the table, bareheaded, she first smiled, and after gave a gawf of laughter. Whereat, when her placeboes gave their *plaudite*, affirming with like countenance, 'This is a good beginning,' she said, 'but wot ye whereat I laugh? Yon man gart me greet [*made me cry*] and grat never tear himself. I will see if I can gar him greet.' At that word the Secretary whispered her in the ear, and she him again, and with that gave him a letter. After the inspection thereof, he directed his visage and speech to John Knox in this manner:—

'The Queen's Majesty is informed, that ye have travailled to raise a tumult of her subjects against her, and for certification thereof, there is presented to her your own letter, subscribed in your name. Yet, because Her Grace will do nothing without a good advisement, she hath convened you before this part of the Nobility, that they may witness betwixt you and her.'

'Let him acknowledge his own handwrit,' said the Queen, 'and then shall we judge the contents of the letter.'

And so was the letter presented from hand to hand to John Knox, who, taking inspection of it, said: 'I gladly acknowledge this to be my handwrit; and also, I remember, I indited a letter in the month of October, giving signification to the Brethren in sundry quarters, of such things as displeased me. And, so good an opinion have I of the fidelity of the scribes that willingly they would not adulterate my original, albeit I left divers blanks subscribed with them, I acknowledge both the handwrit and the inditing.'

*[Later in the proceedings the Queen accused Knox of having made her cry,
and he gives his reply:]*

'Madam, because now the second time Your Grace has
burdened me with that crime, I must answer, lest for my silence I
be holden guilty. If Your Grace be ripely remembered, the Laird
of Dun, yet living to testify the truth, was present at that time
whereof Your Grace complains. Your Grace accused me that I
had irreverently handled you in the pulpit. That I denied. You
said, What ado had I to speak of your marriage? What was I,
touching nature, I was a worm of this earth, and yet a subject of
this Commonwealth; but as touching the office whereinto it had
pleased God to place me, I was a watchman, both over the
Realm and over the Kirk of God gathered within the same; by
reason whereof I was bound in conscience to blow the trumpet
publicly, so oft as ever I saw any appearing danger, either to the
one or to the other. But a certain rumour affirmed that traffic of
marriage was betwixt Your Grace and the Spanish ally.
Thereupon I said, that if your Nobility and Estates did agree,
unless both you and your husband should be so straitly bound,
that neither of you might hurt this Commonwealth, or yet the
pure Kirk of God within the same, that, in that case, I would
pronounce that the consenters were traitors to this Commonwealth, and enemies to God and to His promise planted within
the same. At these words, I grant, Your Grace stormed, and
burst forth into an unreasonable weeping. What mitigation the
Laird of Dun would have made, I suppose Your Grace hath not
forgot. But while nothing was able to stay your weeping, I was
compelled to say:– 'I take God to record, that I never took
pleasure to see any creature weep, yea, not my children when my
own hands had beat them; much less can I rejoice to see Your
Grace make such regret. But, seeing I have offered Your Grace
no such occasion, I must rather suffer Your Grace to take your
own pleasure before I dare conceal the truth, and so betray both
the Kirk of God and my Commonwealth.' These were the most
extreme words that I spoke that day.'

After the Secretary had conferred with the Queen, he said,
'Master Knox, you may return to your house for this night.'

'I thank God and the Queen's Majesty,' said the other. 'And,

Madam, I pray God to purge your heart from Papistry, and to preserve you from the counsel of flatterers; for how pleasant they appear to your ear and corrupt affection for the time, experience hath taught us into what perplexity they have brought famous Princes.'

[37] The coronation of Charles I in the Abbey Church of Holyrood House, 18 June 1633; from *History of the Troubles and Memorable Transactions in Scotland and England from M.DC.XXIV to M.DL.XLV* by John Spalding.

(John Spalding was Clerk to the Consistorial Court of the Diocese of Aberdeen, and was visiting Edinburgh at the time of Charles I's coronation there.)

Upon the morn, Tuesday, [*18 June*], about ten hours in the morning, the nobility came up to the castle in their furred robes, the King had his robe royall, who in order rode from the castle down to the Abbay of Holyroodhouse. And first the earle of Angus (who was made marquess of Douglas the night before) rode immediately before the King in his furred robe, carieing the crown betwixt both his hands, the duke of Lennox being on the King's right hand, and the marquess of Hamiltoun on his left; but before the earle of Angus, rode first the earle of Buchan carieing the sword, and the earle of Rothes carieing the scepter, syde for syde. Thir lords with the rest of the nobility, all richly cled in scarlet furred robes, rode upon their horses, furnished with rich saddles and foot mantles, ilk ane in their own roumes, with the King, down throw the streits to the Abbay; lighted, hard [*heard*] sermon in the Abbay Kirk, preached be Mr David Lindsay, bishop of Breichen, a prime schollar. After sermon the King receives the communion, and some other ceremonies was used as is at the coronation of Kings, and about two, afternoon, his majestie was crowned King of Scotland [*not, as was traditional, King of Scots*], upon the 18th of June 1633. The archbishop of St Andrews, the bishops of Murray, Dunkeld, Ross, Dumblane, and Breichen served about the coronation (which was done be

The Palace of Holyroodhouse; engraving by J.D. Harding *c.*1824

the said bishop of Breichen) with whyt rochetis and whyt sleives, and loops of gold, haveing blue silk to their foot; the bishop of Murray was made lord Elymosinar, who, at the coronation, threw out of his hand, amongst the throng of the people within the Kirk, certain cunzied pieces of silver strucken for that purpose, in token of joy. Now it was remarked, that ther was ane four newcked taffell [*table*], in manner of ane altar, standing within the Kirk, haveing standing therupon two books, at least resembleing clasped books, called *blind books*, with two chandlers and two wax candles, whilk were unlight, and ane bason wherin ther was nothing, at the back of this altar, (covered with tapestrie) there was ane rich tapestrie, wherin the crucifex was curiously wrought; and as the bishops who was in service past by this crucifix, they were sein to bow their knee, and beck, which, with their habite, was notted, and bred great fear of inbringing of poperie, for the whilk they were all deposed, as is sett doun in their papers. The archbishop of Glasgow, and remanent of the bishops there present, who was not in service, changed not their habite; but weir their black gowns, without rochetis, or whyte sleives.

All solemnities done about this coronation, the King goes frae the church, into his own pallace, wher he stays while Thursday the 20th of June, that the haill estates came down to him, who came frae the Abbay in order, (and was the first day of the rydeing of the parliament) as ye shall hear, viz. in the first rank, rode the commissioners of burrows, ilk ane in their own places, weill cled in cloaks, haveing on their horses black velvet foot mantles: 2dly, the commissioners for barrons followed them; 3dly, the lords of the spirituality followed them; 4thly, the bishops, who rode altogither, except the bishop of Aberdein, who was lying sick in Aberdein, and the bishop of Murray, who as Elymosinar rode besyde the bishop of London, somewhat nearer the King; 5thly, followed the temporall lords; 6thly, followed the viscounts; 7thly, the earles followed them; 8thly, the earle of Buchan followed the earles, carieing the sword, and the earle of Rothes, carieing the scepter, rydeing syde for syde with other; 9thly, the marquess of Douglas, careing the crown, haveing on his right arm, the duke of Lennox, and on his left, the marquess of Hamilton, following them; then came his majestie immediately after the marquess of Douglas, rydeing upon ane gallant chesnut collored horse, haveing on his head ane fair bunche of fedders, with ane foot mantle of purpour velvet; as his robe royall was; and none rode but [*without*] their foot mantles, and the nobells all in reid scarlet furred robes, as their use to ryde in parliaments is, but his majestie made choice to ryde in king James the fourth's robe royall, whilk was of pupour velvet, richly furred and laced with gold, hanging over his horse tail ane great deal, whilk was carried up frae the earth, by five grooms of honour, ilk ane after another, all the way as he rode, to his hieness lighting; he had also upon his head ane hatt, and ane rod in his hand. The lyon heraulds, pursevants, macers, and trumpeters, followed his majestie in silence.

[38] The murder of David Riccio (or Rizzio), the Queen's musician, in the Palace of Holyroodhouse, 1566; from *A Relation of the Death of David Rizzio, chief favorite to Mary Stuart Queen of Scotland* by Lord Ruthen.

All this while the King [*Darnley, Mary's husband*] kept secret from the queen's majesty the whole proceedings; and as her majesty sought by subtil means to learn of him what was in his mind, so crafted he with her to seek out her mind: And in the same time he daily sent to the Lord Ruthen; saying that he could not abide Davie [*David Riccio*] any longer; and if his slaughter was not hastened, he would slay him himself, yea though it were in the queen's majesty's own chamber. The said Lord Ruthen counselled him to the contrary, and thought it not decent that he should put hand on such a mean person; yet always the king could not be content, without the said Lord Ruthen affixed a day when the said Davie should be slain. ... In the mean time the king and queen's majesties rode to Seaton; the king so burning in his desire towards the slaughter of David, he sent divers privy writings written in his own hand, and also messages by tongue to George Douglas, to be shewed to the Lord Ruthen, to have all things in readiness against his repairing to Edinburgh towards the slaughter of David, or otherwise he would put the same in execution with his own hands. ... And after the king's return out of Seaton, he directed George Douglas to the Earl of Morton and Lord Ruthen, to see what day should be appointed, with place and time, for the performance of the enterprise against David. The said earl and lord sent answer to the king, and declared they should have a sufficient number ready against Friday or Saturday the 8th or 9th of March to do what he pleased; and enquired of the king what time he would have it the ratherest performed; for according to the said earl's and lord's opinion, they thought it best to take time when David should be in his own chamber in the morning, or in passing through the close: which the king refused *simpliciter*, and said he could not be well taken in his chamber, nor no time in the morning, by reason that at night he tarried late with the queen's majesty; he lay in the over cabinet, and otherwhiles in Signior Francisco's chamber, and sometimes in his own, to which he had sundry backdoors and windows that he might escape at: and if so it were, all were lost. Therefore he would have him taken in the time of the supping, sitting with her majesty at the table, that he might be taken in her own presence; because she had not entertained him her husband according to accustomed manner, nor as she ought of duty. To the which the said earl and lords were very loth to grant, and gave many reasons to the contrary, that it was better to have been done out of her presence, not in the same. Notwithstanding no reason might avail, but the king would have him taken in her majesty's presence, and devised the manner himself, as after followeth: That upon the Saturday at supper-time, the said Earl of Morton, Lord Ruthen, and Lord Lindsey, should have ready so many as would be assistants and partakers with the king, in their houses, against he should send them word; and so soon as he sent them word, that the Earl of Morton should come in, and come up to the queen's utter chamber, and a company with him; and the said Lord Ruthen to come through the king's secret chamber; and that the king should pass up before by a privy passage to the queen's chamber, and open the door, where-through the said Lord Ruthen and his company might enter: and that the king himself should be speaking with the queen's majesty sitting at supper; the remanent barons and gentlemen to be in the court of the palace for keeping of the gates, and defending of the close, in case any of the lords or officers would endeavour to gain-stand the king's enterprize. . . .

Upon Saturday the 9th of March, as is conform to the king's ordenance and device, the said Earl Morton, Lords Ruthen and Lindsey, having their men and friends in readiness, abiding for the king's advertisement; the queen's majesty being in her cabinet within her inner chamber at the supper, the king sent to the said earl and lords, and their complices; and desired them to make haste and come into the palace, for he should have the door of the privy palace open, and should be speaking with the queen before their coming, conform to his device rehearsed before. Then the said Earl of Morton, Lord Ruthen and Lord Lindsey, with their complices, passed up to the queen's utter chamber; and the said Lord Ruthen passed in through the king's chamber, and up through the privy way to the queen's chamber, as the king had learned him, and through the chamber to the cabinet, where he found the queen's majesty sitting at her supper at the middes of a little table, the Lady Argile sitting at one end, and Davie at the head of the table with his cap on his head, the king speaking with the queen's majesty, and his hand about her waste. The said Lord Ruthven at his coming in said to the queen's majesty, It would please your majesty to let yonder man Davie come forth of your presence, for he hath been over-long here. Her majesty answered, What offence hath he made? The said lord replied again, that he had made great offence to her majesty's honour, the king her husband, the nobility and commonweal of the realm. And how? saith she. It will please your majesty, said the said lord, he hath offended your majesty's honour, which I dare not be so bold to speak of: As to the king your husband's honour, he hath hindred him of the crown matrimonial, which your grace promised him, besides many other things which are not necessary to be expressed. And as to the nobility he hath caused your majesty to banish a great part, and most chief thereof, and forefault them at this present parliament, that he might be made a lord. And as to your commonweal, he hath been a common destroyer thereof, in so far as he suffered not your majesty to grant or give any thing but that which passed through his hands, by taking of bribes and goods for the same; and caused your majesty to put out the Lord Ross from his whole lands, because he would not give the lordship of Melvin to the said Davie; besides many other inconveniences that he sollicited your majesty to do. Then the said Lord Ruthen said to the king, Sir, take the queen's majesty your sovereign and wife to you, who stood all amazed, and wyst not what to do. Then her majesty rose on her feet and stood before Davie, he holding her majesty by the plates of the gown, leaning back over in the window, his whiniard drawn in his hand. Arthur Erskin and the abbot of Holyroodhouse, the laird of Crech, master of the household, and one of the grooms of the chamber, began to lay hands upon the said Lord Ruthen, none of the king's party being present. Then the said lord pulled out his whiniard, and freed himself while more came in, and said to them, Lay not hands on me, for I will not be handled; and at the incoming of others into the cabinet, the said Lord Ruthen put up his whiniard. And with the rushing in of men the board fell to the wallwards, with meat and candles being thereon; and the Lady Argile took up one of the candles in her hand: and in the same instant the said Lord Ruthen took the queen in his arms, and put her into the king's arms, beseeching her majesty not to be afraid, for there was no man there that would do her majesty's body more harm than their own hearts; and assured her majesty, all that was done was the king's deed and action. Then the remanent gentlemen being in the cabinet, took Davie out of the window; and after that they had him out in the queen's chamber, the said Lord Ruthen followed, and bad take him down the privy way to the king's chamber, as said is; but the press of the people hurl'd him forth to the utter chamber, where there was a great number standing, who were so vehemently moved against the said Davie, that they could not abide any longer, but slew him at the queen's far door in the utter chamber. Immediately the Earl of Morton passed forth of the queen's majesty's utter chamber to the inner court, for keeping of the same and the gates, and deputed certain barons to keep Davie's chamber till he knew the queen's majesty's pleasure, and the king's. . . . In this mean time the queen's majesty and the king came forth of the cabinet to the queen's chamber, where her majesty began to reason with the king, saying, my lord, why have you caused to do this wicked deed to me, considering I took you from a base estate, and made you my husband? what offence have I made you that ye should have done me such shame? The king answered and said, I have good reason for me: for since yon fellow Davie fell in credit and familiarity with your majesty, ye regarded me not, neither treated me nor entertained me after your wonted fashion; for every day before dinner, and after dinner, ye would come to my chamber and pass time with me, and thus long time ye have not done so; and when I came to your majesty's chamber, ye bear me little company, except Davie had been the third marrow: and after supper your majesty hath a use to set at cards with the said Davie till one or two of the clock after midnight; and this is the entertainment that I have had of you this long time. Her majesty's answer was, It was not gentlewomens duty to come to their husband's chamber, but rather the husband to come to the wive's chamber, if he had any thing to do with her. The king answered, How came ye to my chamber at the beginning, and ever, till within these few months that Davie fell in familiarity with you? or am I failed in any sort of my body? or what disdain have you at me? seeing that I am willing to do all things that becometh a good husband to do to his wife. For since you have chose me to be your husband, suppose I be of the baser degree, yet I am your head, and ye promised obedience at the day of our marriage, and that I should be equal with you, and participant in all things. I suppose you have used me otherwise by the perswasions of Davie. Her majesty answered and said, that all the shame that was done to her, that my lord ye have the weight thereof; for the which I shall never be your wife, nor lie with you; nor shall never like well, till I gar you have as sore a heart as I have presently.

[39] James VII fits out the Abbey Church, Holyrood, as a Roman Catholic chapel, 1687; from *Chronological Notes of Scottish Affairs from 1680 till 1701* by Sir John Lauder of Fountainhall.

(Sir John Lauder, 1646–1722, Scottish landowner and judge, was both a strong Presbyterian and a committed Royalist.)

There was a letter frae the King, bearing that the Abbey Church was the chappell belonging to his palace of Holyroodhouse, and that the Knights of the Order of the Thistle, or St Andrews, which he had now errected, could not meet in St Andrews Church, (being demolished in the rebellion, as they called our Reformation, which in effect was no less than a deformation, by casting down many religious places.) . . . And so this church was necessar for his Majesty to have; and the Provost of Edinburgh wes ordained to sie the keyes thereof given to them. So this is the first Protestant church taken away from us, and was also the last. 12th July, 1687.

[40] The mob purges the Abbey Church of its Roman Catholic ornaments, December 1688; from *Memorials of Edinburgh in the Olden Time* by Sir Daniel Wilson.

The news of the arrival of the Prince of Orange filled the Presbyterian party in Scotland with the utmost joy. The Earl of Perth, who was chancellor, hastily quitted Edinburgh, and the mob made it the signal for an attack on Holyrood Chapel. A body of a hundred men defended it with firearms, which they freely used against their assailants, killing twelve of them and wounding many more. But this only increased the fury of the mob; the armed defenders were at length overpowered, and the chapel delivered up to their will. The magnificent carved stalls, which had just been completed, and all the costly fittings of the chapel, were reduced to an unsightly heap of ruins. Other acts of violence were perpetrated by the rioters; and the students again testified their zeal by marching in triumphal procession to the [*Mercat*] Cross, with bands of music, and the College mace borne before them, and there again burning the effigy of the Pope.

[41] Bonnie Prince Charlie in Holyrood, 1745; from *The History of the Rebellion in the Year 1745* by John Home.

About ten o'clock the main body of the rebels marching by Duddingston (to avoid being fired upon by the Castle) entered the King's Park, and halted in the hollow between the hills, under the peak called Arthur's Seat. By and by Charles came down to the Duke's Walk, accompanied by the Highland Chiefs, and other commanders of his army.

The Park was full of people, (amongst whom was the Author of this history), all of them impatient to see this extraordinary person. The figure and presence of Charles Stuart were not ill suited to his lofty pretensions. He was in the prime of youth, tall and handsome, of a fair complexion; he had a light coloured periwig with his own hair combed over the front: he wore the Highland dress, that is a tartan short coat without the plaid, a blue bonnet on his hend, and on his breast the star of the order of St. Andrew. Charles stood some time in the park to shew himself to the people; and then, though he was very near the palace, mounted his horse, either to render himself more conspicuous, or because he rode well, and looked graceful on horseback.

The Jacobites were charmed with his appearance: they compared him to Robert the Bruce, whom he resembled (they said) in his figure as in his fortune. The Whigs looked upon him with other eyes. They acknowledged that he was a goodly person: but they observed, that even in that triumphant hour, when he was about to enter the palace of his fathers, the air of his countenance was languid and melancholy: that he looked like a gentleman and a man of fashion, but not like a hero or a conqueror. Hence they formed their conclusions that the enterprize was above the pitch of his mind; and that his heart was not great enough for the sphere in which he moved. When Charles came to the palace, he dismounted, and walked along the piazza, towards the apartment of the Duke of Hamilton. When he was near the door, which stood open to receive him, a gentleman stepped out of the crowd, drew his sword, and raising his arm aloft, walked up stairs before Charles. The person who enlisted himself in this manner, was James Hepburn of Keith, whose name will be mentioned again more than once; he had been engaged when a very young man in the rebellion of the year 1715, and from that time (learned and intelligent as he was) had continued a Jacobite. But he had compounded the spirit of Jacobitism with another spirit; for he disclaimed the hereditary indefeasible right of Kings, and condemned the government of James the Second; but he also condemned the Union between England and Scotland, as injurious, and humiliating to his Country; saying, (to use his own words), that the Union had made a Scotch gentleman of small fortune nobody, and that he would die a thousand times rather than submit to it.

[42] Charles X of France in Holyrood; from *Kay's Edinburgh Portraits, Written by James Paterson and Edited by James Maidment.*

(The exiled Comte d'Artois, Charles Philippe, came to Edinburgh in 1796 and resided at the Palace of Holyroodhouse. On 16 September 1824 he succeeded his brother Louis XVIII to become Charles X of France. He lost his throne in the July revolution of 1830 and returned to Holyrood.

James Kay, 1742–1826, was a caricaturist, engraver and miniature painter whose caricatures of Edinburgh worthies were accompanied by biographical sketches by the Scottish antiquary James Paterson. This is from Paterson's text accompanying Kay's caricature of the duc d'Angoulême, Charles X's oldest son, who accompanied him during both periods of his residence at Holyrood.)

On quitting the shores of France, Charles X, then in his seventy-third year, appears to have at once contemplated returning to the Palace of Holyrood – the scene of his former exile, and where he had experienced many years of comparative happiness. With this view, he applied to the British Govermnent, which granted the permission solicited; and after a short residence in England, he arrived at Edinburgh on the 20th of October, 1830. He and his suite, including the young Duc de Bordeaux and the Duc de Polignac, were conveyed from Poole in an Admiralty yacht, and landed at Newhaven. The ex-king not having been expected for several days, there were few people on the beach. By those assembled, however, he was received with a degree of respect scarcely to have been expected in the then excited state of the public mind. Amongst those that pressed forward to bid him welcome was a jolly Newhaven fishwoman, who, pushing every one aside, seized the hand of the King as he was about to enter his carriage, and, with hearty shake, exclaimed, 'Oh,sir, I'm happy

to see ye again among decent folk.' Charles smiled, and asking
her name, she replied, 'My name's Kirsty Ramsay, sir, and mony
a guid fish I ha'e gi'en ye, sir; and mony a guid shilling I ha'e got
for't thirty years sin syne.'

On the Saturday following his arrival, a dinner was given to
between thirty and forty respectable citizens, by several of the
ex-monarch's old tradesmen, in honour of his return to Edinburgh. The entertainment took place in Johnston's Tavern,
Abbey. After dinner, the party repaired to the Palace Square,
and serenaded its inhabitants with 'Should auld acquaintance
be forgot', which was excellently sung in parts by about twenty
individuals. Three cheers followed the conclusion of the song.

[43] Whisky at the Palace of Holyroodhouse, during the
visit of George IV to Scotland in 1822 (the first by any
reigning monarch since James VII in the late seventeenth
century); from *Memoirs of a Highland Lady 1797–1827* by
Elizabeth Grant of Rothiemurchus.

Lord Conyngham, the Chamberlain, was looking everywhere
for pure Glenlivet whisky; the King drank nothing else. It was
not to be had out of the Highlands. My father sent word to me – I
was the cellarer – to empty my pet bin, where was whisky long in
wood, long in uncorked bottles, mild as milk, and the true
contraband *goût* in it. Much as I grudged this treasure it made
our fortunes afterwards, showing on what trifles great events
depend. The whisky, and fifty brace of ptarmigan all shot by one
man, went up to Holyrood House, and were graciously received
and made much of, and a reminder of this attention at a proper
moment by the gentlemanly Chamberlain ensured to my father
the Indian judgeship.

The entry of George IV into Holyroodhouse in 1822; by David Wilkie

The High Kirk of St Giles

[44] John Knox first preached at St Giles in 1559, at a time when Mary Queen of Scots, with her French Catholic supporters, was opposed by the anti-Catholic Presbyterians; from *The History of the Reformation in Scotland* by John Knox.

For the comfort of the Brethren, and continuance of the Kirk in Edinburgh, was left there our dear brother John Willock, who, for his faithful labours and bold courage in that battle, deserveth immortal praise. For when it was found dangerous that John Knox, who before [*on 7th July 1559*] was elected minister to that church, should continue there, the Brethren requested the said John Willock to abide with them, lest that, for lack of ministers, idolatry should be erected up again. To the which he so gladly consented, that it might evidently appear, that he preferred the comfort of his Brethren, and the continuance of the church there, to his own life. One part of the Frenchmen was appointed to lie in garrison at Leith – that was the first benefit they got for their confederacy with them – the other part was appointed to lie in the Canongate; the Queen and her train abiding in the Abbey. Our brother John Willock, the day after our departure, preached in St Giles Kirk, and fervently exhorted the Brethren to stand constant in the Truth which they had professed. At this and some other sermons were the Duke and divers others of the Queen's faction. This liberty and preaching, with resort of all people thereto, did highly offend the Queen and the other Papists. First, they began to give terrors to the Duke; affirming, that he would be repute as one of the Congregation, if he gave his presence to the sermons. Thereafter they began to require that Mass should be set up again in St Giles Kirk, and the people should be set at liberty to choose what religion they would; for that – say they – was contained in the Appointment, that the town of Edinburgh should choose what religion they list. . . .

After many persuasions and threatenings made by the said

Earl and Lord, the Brethren, stoutly and valiantly in the Lord Jesus, gainsaid their most unjust petitions, reasoning: 'That as of conscience they might not suffer idolatry to be erected where Christ Jesus was truly preached, so could not the Queen nor they require any such thing, unless she and they would plainly violate their faith and the chief article of the Appointment; for it is plainly appointed, That no member of the Congregation shall be molested in any thing that, at the day of the Appointment, he peaceably possessed. But so it was that we, the Brethren and Protestants of the town of Edinburgh, with our ministers, the day of the Appointment, did peaceably possess St Giles Kirk, appointed for us for preaching of Christ's true Evangel, and right administration of His Holy Sacraments. Therefore, without manifest violation of the Appointment, ye cannot remove us therefrom, until a Parliament have decided this controversy.'

This answer given, the whole Brethren departed and left the foresaid Earl, and Lord Seton, then Provost of Edinburgh, still in the Tolbooth. They, perceiving that they could not prevail in that matter, began to entreat that they would be quiet, and that they would so far condescend to the Queen's pleasure, as that they would choose them another kirk within the town, or at the least be contented that Mass should be said either before or after their sermons. To the which, answer was given: 'That to give place to the Devil, who was the chief inventor of the Mass, for the pleasure of any creature, they could not. They were in possession of that kirk, which they could not abandon; neither could they suffer idolatry to be erected in the same unless by violence they should be constrained to do so; and then they were determined to seek the next remedy.'

[45] St Giles in 1598; from *An Itinerary written by Fynes Moryson, gent.*

In the midst of the foresaid faire streete, the Cathedrall Church is built, which is large and lightesome, but little stately for the building, and nothing at all for the beauty and ornament. In this Church the Kings seate is built some few staires high of wood,

The northern prospect of St Giles's Church, the High Kirk; by
Fourdrinier, 1753

and leaning upon the pillar next to the Pulpit: And opposite to
the same is another seat very like it, in which the incontinent use
to stand and doe penance; and some few weekes past, a
Gentleman, being a stranger, and taking it for a place wherein
Men of better quality used to sit, boldly entred the same in
Sermon time, till he was driven away with the profuse laughter of
the common sort, to the disturbance of the whole Congregation.

[46] The protest in St Giles on 23 July 1637 against the
imposition of Archbishop Laud's new service book; from *A
Relation of the Proceedings concerning the Affairs of the Kirk of
Scotland* by John, Earl of Rothes.
(There are many traditional stories about the riotous protest in
St Giles against the new service book, regarded as 'Popish' by the
Presbyterians; a popular one is that a woman called Jenny
Geddes threw a stool at either the Dean of Edinburgh or the
Bishop (Edinburgh's first bishop, David Lindsay) saying 'Durst

thou say Mass in my lug [ear]?' But the only contemporary
account is less picturesque.)

This book [*the new service book*], long keipit up in misterie, begane
to be discovered als soon as published and put to seall. The
Bischops, not yit apprehending how much the people abhorred
poperie, did enjoyne the practise of the book in their severall
synods; and the Bischop of Edinburgh (who had given to some of
his ministers whill the next synod to examine it) did resolve,
within a fortnight therefter of this new piece of episcopall
begetting, by himselfe, in the great church of Edinburgh (the
principall citie in this land), on the 23 July last. The lyke was
intendit in other churches in that town, efter publict
intimationne (yit without a publict determinatione of any
particular day for practise)by the ministers on the Sabboth
preceding. These people, formerly patient under all uther new
devyces that wer brought in by degrees, wer unable to bear at
ane instant so great a change as appeired, in the mater, to those of
best understanding, and, in the maner and forme, to the weakest,
even to change the whole externall frame of Gods publict
worschip formerlie practised. This alteratione of religione
appearing so sensible to the hearts, eyes and ears (the greatest
cause under heaven of discontent), the unwarrantable
introductione thereof, and superstitious mater contained therein, the fear that their own lawfull service once dispossessed wold
hardlie be repossessed, and that new illegall service being
permitted to take footing and possessione it wold hardlie be
removed, and the means of remedie seiming to be closed up from
the Magistrats who had consented, from the Bischops who wer
repute authors, from his Majestie, by whose authoritie abused it
was imposed, and betuixt whose favour and them stood a great
many misinformers, whose conditione preferred them to better
hearing and trust, made sum out of zeall, sum out of griefe, and
sum from astonishment at such a change, vent their words and
cryes, that stayed the said service to be red that forenoon. Sum
Bischops and Ministers, efter the ordinarie time of divyne service
in the afternoon, returneing privatlie, and with closed doores
intending the practise thereof, as it wer by possessione to give lyfe

and being to that unlawfull service, provocked a number of the Commons (who believed the Service to be Masse, which they had alwayes bein taught by the lawes of the countrey and sermons of their pastors formerlie to distaste and resist) to cry out, and, it is alleged, to throw stones at the Bischops.

Parliament Square,
Parliament Close,
Parliament House (or Hall)

[47] The 'riding' of the Scottish Parliament – the old fuedal ceremony of riding in procession from Holyrood to Parliament House – in 1669; from *Travels over England, Scotland and Wales* by James Brome.

(Brome was a clergyman of the Church of England who visited Scotland in 1669.)

Not far from the cathedral is the Parliament House, whither we had the good fortune to see all the flower of the nobility then to pass in state, attending Duke Lauderdale who was sent down High-Commissioner. And indeed it was a very glorious sight, for they were all richly accoutred and as nobly attended with a splendid retinue, the heralds of arms and other officers, that went before were wonderful gay and finely habited, and the servants that attended were clad in the richest liveries; their coaches drawn with six horses, as they went ratling along, did dazle our eyes with the splendour of their furniture, and all the nobles appeared in the greatest pomp and gallantry; the regalia, which are the sword of state, the scepter, and the crown were carried by three of the antientest of the nobility, and on each side the honours were three mace-bearers bare headed, a nobleman bare headed with a purse, and in it the Lord High Commissioner's commission, then last of all the Lord High Commissioner with the dukes and marquesses on his right and left hand: it is ordered that there be no shooting under the highest penalties that day, neither displaying of ensigns, nor beating of drums during the whole cavalcade: The officers of state not being noblemen, ride in their gowns, all the members ride covered except those that carry the honours, and the highest degree and the most honourable of that degree ride last.

[48] The women of Edinburgh present a petition, 4 June 1672; from *The Secret and True History of the Church of Scotland from the Restoration to the year 1678* by James Kirkton.

(Kirkton, c. 1620–1699, was a Covenanting minister who had to flee to Holland after denunciation as a rebel for holding conventicles; he returned to Scotland in 1687 and became minister of the Tolbooth parish. His historical work was left in manuscript and not published until 1817.)

Also this summer, because men durst not, the women of Edinburgh would needs appeal in a petition to the councill, wherein they desired a gospell ministry might be provided for the starving congregations of Scotland. Fifteen of them, most part ministers' widows, engadged to present so many copies to the principal lords of councill, and upon the 4th of June filled the whole Parliament Closse. When the chancellor came up, Sharp [*James Sharp, Archbishop of St Andrews, who was murdered by extremist Covenanters in 1679*] came up with him, and as the chancellor left his coach, Sharp clapt closse to his back, fearing, it may be, bodily harm, which he then escapt; only some of them reproached him, calling him Judas and traitor, and one of them laid her hand upon his neck, and told him that neck must pay for it ere all was done, and in that guessed right; ... Mr John Livingston's widow undertook to present her copie to the chancellor, which she did. He received it, and civilly pul't off his hat. Then she begane to speak, and took hold of his sleeve. He bowed down his head and listened to her (because she spake well), even till he came to the councill chamber door. She who presented her copy to Stair [*Sir James Dalrymple, first Viscount Stair, jurist and statesman*] found no such kind reception, for he threw it upon the ground. ... But when the councill conveened, the petition was turned into a seditious lybell in the vote of the court. The provest and guard were sent for, but none of these

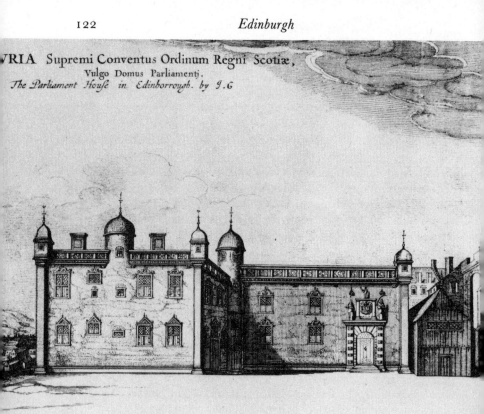

VRIA Supremi Conventus Ordinum Regni Scotiæ,
Vulgo Domus Parliamentj.
The Parliament House in Edinborrough. by J.G

Parliament House *c.*1649; by James Gordon

were very cruell; only they threatned, and the women dissolved.
Thereafter for ane example some of them were cited, and some
denunced rebels. Three women they incarcerate also for a time.
... and this was the end of that brush.

[49] The last 'riding' of the Scottish Parliament, 6 May
1703; from the Appendix to *The History of Edinburgh* by
Hugo Arnot.

The streets of the city of Edinburgh and Canongate being
cleared of all coaches and carriages, and a lane formed, by the

streets being inrailed, on both sides; within which none were permitted to enter but those who went in procession, the captains, lieutenants, and ensigns of the trained bands excepted. Without the rails, the streets being lined with the horse guards, from the palace of Holyrood-house, westwards; after them with the horse grenadiers; next, with the foot guards who covered the streets up to the Netherbow; and thence to the Parliament Square, by the trained bands of the city; from the Parliament Square to the Parliament House, by the Lord High Constable's guards; and from the Parliament House to the bar, by the Earl Marshall's guards; the Lord High Constable being seated in an elbow-chair at the door of the Parliament House; the officers of state having rode up before in their robes; and the members of parliament, with their attendants, being assembled at Holyrood-house, the rolls of parliament were called by the Lord Register, Lord Lyon, and Heralds, from the windows and gates of the palace; from which the procession moved to the Parliament House in the following order:

Two trumpets in coats and banners, bareheaded, riding.
Two pursuivants in coats and foot-mantles, ditto.
Sixty-three commissioners for boroughs on horseback,
covered, two and two, each having a lacquey
attending on foot, the odd member
walking alone.
Seventy-seven commissioners for shires on horseback,
covered, two and two,
each having two lackies attending on foot.
Fifty-one Lords Barons in their robes, riding,
two and two,
each having a gentleman to support his train, and three
lackies on foot, wearing above their liveries, velvet
surtouts, with the arms, of their respective lords,
on the breast and back, embossed on plate,
or embroidered with gold and silver.
Nineteen Viscounts as the former.
Sixty Earls as the former, four lackies attending on each
Four trumpets, two and two.
Four pursuivants, two and two.

And six heralds, two and two, bareheaded.
Lord Lyon King at Arms, in his coat, robe, chain, batoon,
and foor-mantle.
Sword of State
borne by the Earl of Marr,
The Sceptre,
by the Earl of Crawfurd.
THE CROWN
By the Earl of Forfar, in room of the Marquis of Douglas.
The Purse and Commission, by the
Earl of Morton.
The DUKE OF QUEENSBERRY, LORD HIGH COMMISSIONER,
with his servants, pages
and footmen.
Four Dukes, two and two,
Gentlemen bearing their trains,
and each having eight lackies.
Six Marquisses,
each having six lackies.
The Duke of Argyle.
Captain of the Horse Guards.
The Horse Guards.

[50] Riots against the Union in 1706; from *Memoirs Concerning the Affairs of Scotland* by George Lockhart of Carnwath.

(George Lockhart was a fiercely anti-Union Jacobite, who nevertheless served as Member of Parliament for Edinburgh 1708–1715, but was arrested as a Jacobite during the Jacobite rising of 1715 and later fled to Holland.)

During this Time, the Nation's Aversion to the Union increased; the Parliament Close, and the outer Parliament House, were crowded every Day when the Parliament was met, with an infinite Number of People, all exclaiming against the Union, and speaking very free Language concerning the Promoters of it. The

Commissioner, as he passed along the Street, was cursed and reviled to his Face, and the D[uke] of H[amilto]n huzza'd and convey'd every Night, with a great Number of Apprentices and younger Sort of People, from the Parliament House to the Abbey, exhorting him to stand by the Country and assuring him of his being supported. And upon the Twenty Third of Octob.[*1706*] above Three or Four Hundred of them being thus employ'd, did, as soon as they left his Grace, hasten in a Body to the House of Sir *Pat. Johnston* (their late darling Provost, one of the Commissioners of the Treaty, a great Promoter of the Union, in Parliament, where he sat as one of the Representatives of the Town of *Edinburg*) threw Stones at his Windows, broke open his Doors, and search'd his House for him, but he having narrowly made his Escape, prevented his being torn in a Thousand Pieces. From thence the Mob, which was encreas'd to a great Number, went thro' the Streets, threatning Destruction on to all the Promoters of the Union, and continu'd for four or five Hours in this Temper; till about three next Morning, a strong Detachment of the Foot Guards was sent to secure the Gate call'd the *Netherbow Port*, and keep Guard in the Parliament Close.

[51] After four years of fierce debate, the Scottish Parliament finally votes for an 'incorporating union' with England on 16 January 1707; from *Minutes of the Proceedings in Parliament.*

Draught of the Act *Ratifying and Approving the Treaty of Union of the two Kingdoms of* Scotland *and* England, Read a second time.

Then the Act for *Security of the Protestant Religion and Presbyterian Church Government,* which is insert in and Ratifyed by the above Act, was touched with the Royal Scepter by her Majesties high Commissioner in the usual manner.

Representation and Petition of the Commission of the General Assembly of the Church of *Scotland* given in and Read.

And after Reasoning upon the Act and Representation, the Vote was stated, *Approve the Act or Not.*

And before Voteing, It was agreed, That the Members votes

be marked, and that the List of their Names as they vote be printed and Recorded, and the Lord high Chancellor was allowed to have his Name Marked, Printed and Recorded as an Approver. . . .

Then the Vote was put, *Approve the Act Ratifying and Approving the Treaty of Union of the two Kingdoms of* Scotland *and England, Yea or Not,* and it carried *Approve.*

And the Act was thereafter Touched with the Royal Scepter by Her Majesties high Commissioner in the usual manner.

[52] After the Union the Scottish Parliament ceased to exist, and Parliament Hall became part of the Scottish Law Courts which later moved to adjacent new buildings to the east of Parliament Hall (still in Parliament Square); from *Memorials of His Time,* by Lord Cockburn.

(Henry Thomas Cockburn, 1779–1854, successively Solicitor General and Lord of Session, as Lord Cockburn – the Court of Session was and is the supreme court in Scotland in civil cases – kept an account of his life and times, which, like his Journal, was published posthumously.)

The modern accommodation for the courts is so ample that it is curious to recollect its amount, and how it looked before 1808, when the judges began to sit in two separate chambers. The den called The Inner House then held the whole fifteen judges. It was a low square-like room, not, I think, above from thirty to forty feet wide. It stood just off the south-east corner of the Outer House; with the Exchequer, entering from the Parliament Close, right above. The Barons being next the sky, had access to the flat leaden roof, where I have seen my father, who was one of them [*i.e., one of the Barons of the Exchequer*], walking in his robes. The Inner House was so cased in venerable dirt that it was impossible to say whether it had ever been painted; but it was all of a dark brownish hue. There was a gallery over the bar, and so low that a barrister in a frenzy was in danger of hitting it. A huge fire-place stood behind the Lord President's chair, with one of the stone jambs cracked, and several of the bars of the large grate broken. That grate was always at least half full of dust. It probably had never been completely cleared since the institution of the Court in the sixteenth century. The hearth-stone, the fender, and the chimney-piece were all massive, and all undisturbed by any purification. On the one side of that fire-place there was fixed in a wooden frame the Lord's Prayer, and on the other side the Ten Commandments; each worked in faded gold-thread letters into a black velvet ground. George Cranstoun used to propose adding a scriptural verse to be set over the head of each judge, and had culled the texts.

Dismal though this hole was, the old fellows who had been bred there never looked so well anywhere else; and deeply did they growl at the spirit of innovation which drove them from their accustomed haunts.

The Lawnmarket

[53] William Brodie, Deacon of Wrights and Masons of Edinburgh, had a thriving business as a cabinet-maker in the Lawnmarket, but he led a very different life at night; from *Kay's Edinburgh Portraits*.

The trial of this individual for breaking into the Excise Office (then in Chessels's Court, Canongate), on the 5th March, 1788, created an unprecedented excitement in Edinburgh, arising not only from the extent and aggravated nature of the burglary, but from the respectable sphere of life in which the criminal previously moved. . . .

About the latter end of 1787, a series of robberies were committed in and around Edinburgh, and no clue could be had of the perpetrators. Shops were opened, and goods disappeared as if by magic. The whole city at last became alarmed. An old lady mentions that a female friend of her's, who, from indisposition, was unable to go one Sunday to church, was, during divine worship, and in the absence of the servant, surprised by the entrance of a man, with a crape over his face, into the room where she was sitting. He very coolly took up the keys which were lying on the table before her, opened her bureau, and took out a considerable sum of money that had been placed there. He meddled with nothing else, but immediately re-locked the bureau, replaced the keys on the table, and, making a low bow, retired. The lady was panic-struck the whole time. Upon the exit of her mysterious visitor, she exclaimed, 'Surely that was Deacon Brodie!' But the improbability of a person of his opulence turning a housebreaker, induced her to preserve silence at the time. Subsequent events, however, soon proved the truth of her surmises. In the most of these Brodie was either actively or passively concerned; but it was not until the last 'fatal affair' – the robbery of the Excise Office – that he was discovered, and the whole machinery laid open.

This undertaking, it appears, was wholly suggested and

St Giles, County Hall, and the Lawnmarket; by Thomas Shepherd
from *Modern Athens . . .*, 1829

planned by Brodie. A friend of his, a Mr Corbett from Stirling,
had occasion to visit the Excise Office for the purpose of drawing
money. Brodie accompanied him; and, while in the cashier's
room, the idea first occurred to him. He immediately acquainted
his colleagues with the design, and frequently made calls at the
office, under the pretence of asking for Mr Corbett, but with the
sole purpose of becoming better acquainted with the premises.
On one of those visits, in company with Smith, he observed the
key of the outer door hanging on a nail, from which he took an
impression of the wards with putty; and on the night of the 30th
November, with the key formed from this model, they opened
the outer door by way of experiment, but proceeded no farther.

It was not till the 5th of March following that the final attempt was made; on which occasion all hands were engaged. Their plan of procedure was previously well-concerted, and their tools prepared. They were to meet in the house of Smith about seven o'clock; but Brodie did not appear till eight, when he came dressed in an old-fashioned suit of black, and armed with a brace of pistols. He seemed in high spirits for the adventure, and was chanting the well-known ditty from the 'Beggars' Opera' –

'Let us take the road,
Hark! I hear the sound of coaches!
The hour of attack approaches;
To your arms, brave boys, and load.
See the ball I hold;
Let the chemists toil like asses –
Our fire their fire surpasses,
And turns our lead to gold.'

Brodie also brought with him some small keys and a double picklock. Particular duties were assigned to each. Ainslie was to keep watch in the courtyard; Brodie inside the outer door; while Smith and Brown were to enter the cashier's room. The mode of giving alarm was by means of a whistle, bought by Brodie the day before, with which Ainslie was to call once, if only one person approached – if two or more, he was to call thrice, and then proceed himself to the back of the building to assist Brown and Smith in escaping by the windows. All of them, save Ainslie, were armed with pistols. Brown and Smith had pieces of crape over their faces. They chose the hour of attack from the circumstances of the office being generally shut at eight, and no watchman being stationed till ten. . . .

The robbery having been discovered about ten o'clock the same night it was committed, the town was in consternation, and the police on the alert in all directions. . . .

Brodie, suspecting he stood on ticklish ground, fled on Sunday morning and, from the masterly manner in which he accomplished his escape, baffled all pursuit for a time. On the Wednesday following, Mr Williamson, King's messenger for

Scotland, was despatched in search of him. He traced Brodie to Dunbar and Newcastle, and afterwards to London: from thence Williamson went to Margate, Deal, and Dover, but lost sight of him altogether; and, after eighteen days' fruitless search, returned to Edinburgh. But for Brodie's own imprudence, impelled apparently by a sort of fatuity frequently evinced by persons similarly situated, there was every chance of his finally escaping. He remained in London, it appears, until the 23rd March, when he took out his passage, in the name of John Dixon, on board one of the smacks bound for Leith, called the *Endeavour*. After the vessel had gone down the river Thames, Brodie came on board in a small boat, about twelve o'clock at night, disguised as an old gentleman in bad health. He was accompanied by two of the owners, who stopped on board for a short time. On going out to sea, as it no doubt had been previously arranged, the *Endeavour* steered for Flushing instead of Leith, where Brodie was put ashore, and immediately after took a Dutch skiff for Ostend.

So far so well: but, unfortunately for Brodie, there had been a Mr Geddes, tobacconist in Mid-Calder, and his wife, fellow-passengers, with whom he frequently entered into conversation. On parting, he had given Geddes three letters to deliver in Edinburgh – one addressed to his brother-in-law, Matthew Sherriff, upholsterer; another to Michael Henderson, Grassmarket; and the third to Ann Grant, Cant's Close, Brodie's favourite mistress. She had three children to him. These letters, as he might well have expected, were the means of his discovery. On landing at Leith, Geddes became acquainted with the circumstances of the robbery, and immediately suspecting that Mr John Dixon was no other than Deacon Brodie, he opened the letters, and became doubly strengthened in his opinion; but not having made up his mind how to proceed, Mr Geddes did not deliver the letters to the authorities till near the end of May. Even then, however, they were the means of Brodie's apprehension, and were afterwards put in evidence against him. Information of the circumstances was instantly despatched to Sir John Potter, British Consul at Ostend, in consequence of which Brodie was traced to Amsterdam, where, on application to Sir James Harris, then Consul, he was apprehended in an alehouse, through the instrumentality of one Daly, an Irishman, on the eve of his departure to America, and lodged in the Stadthouse. A Mr Groves, messenger, was despatched from London; and from thence to Edinburgh by Mr Williamson, who was specially sent up to take charge of him. On the journey from London Brodie was in excellent spirits, and told many anecdotes of his sojourn in Holland.

The trial took place in the High Court of Justiciary, on the 27th August, 1788, before Lords Hailes, Eskgrove, Stonefield, and Swinton. The Court from the great excitement in the public mind, was crowded to excess at an early hour. Smith and Brodie only were indicted, the other two having become 'king's evidence'. The trial commenced at nine o'clock in the morning of the following day. All the facts we have previously narrated were fully borne out by the evidence, as well as by the declarations of Smith while in prison. An attempt was made to prove an *alibi* on the part of Brodie, by means of Jean Watt and her maid; but the jury, 'all in one voice', returned a verdict finding both panels 'guilty'. They were sentenced, therefore, to be executed at the west end of the Luckenbooths, on Wednesday, the 1st October, 1788.

The following account of the execution we give from one of the periodicals of the day:– 'About a quarter-past two, the criminals appeared on the platform, preceded by two of the magistrates in their robes, with white staves, and attended by the Rev. Mr Hardy, one of the ministers of Edinburgh – the Rev. Mr Cleeve, of the Episcopal persuasion, in their gowns, and the Rev. Mr Hall, of the Burghers. When Mr Brodie came to the scaffold, he bowed politely to the magistrates and the people. He had on a full suit of black – his hair dressed and powdered. Smith was dressed in white linen, trimmed with black. Having spent some time in prayer, with seeming fervence, with the clergymen, Mr Brodie then prayed a short time by himself.

'Having put on white nightcaps, Brodie pointed to Smith to ascend the steps that led to the drop, and, in an easy manner, clapping him on the shoulder, said, "George Smith, you are first in hand." Upon this Smith, whose behaviour was highly penitent and resigned, slowly ascended the steps, and was immediately followed by Brodie, who mounted with briskness and agility, and examined the dreadful apparatus with attention, and particularly the halter designed for himself. The ropes being too short tied, Brodie stepped down to the platform again, but the rope was still too short; and he once more descended to the platform, showing some impatience. During this dreadful interval Smith remained on the drop with great composure and placidness. Brodie having ascended a third time, and the rope being at last properly adjusted, he deliberately untied his neckcloth, buttoned up his waistcoat and coat, and helped the executioner to fix the rope. He then took a friend (who stood close by him) by the hand, bade him farewell, and requested that he would acquaint the world that he was still the same, and that he died like a man. He then pulled the nightcap over his face, and placed himself in an attitude expressive of firmness and resolution. Smith, who, during all this time had been in fervent devotion, let fall a handkerchief as a signal, and a few minutes before three they were launched into eternity. Brodie on the scaffold neither confessed nor denied his being guilty. Smith, with great fervency, confessed in prayer his being guilty, and the justice of his sentence, and showed in all his conduct the proper expressions of penitence, humility, and faith. This execution was conducted with more than usual solemnity; and the great bell tolled during the ceremony, which had an awful and solemn effect. The crowd of spectators was immense.'

Kirk o' Field

[54] The murder of Darnley, 10 February 1567; from
Traditions of Edinburgh by Robert Chambers.

(Henry Stewart, Lord Darnley, married Mary Queen of Scots in
1565, but she soon became disillusioned with his arrogance,
petulance and dissipation: whether Mary was a party to his
murder is still in dispute. Kirk o' Field stood where the Old
College of Edinburgh now stands, on South Bridge.)

While this event is connected with one of the most problematical
points in our own history, or that of any other nation, it chances
that the whole topography of the affair is very distinctly
recorded. We know not only the exact spot where the deed was
perpetrated, but almost every foot of the ground over which the
perpetrators walked on their way to execute it. It is chiefly by
reason of the depositions and confessions brought out by the legal
proceedings against the inferior instruments, that this minute
knowledge is attained.

The house in which the unfortunate victim resided at the time
was one called the Prebendaries' Chamber, being part of the
suite of domestic buildings connected with the collegiate church
of St-Mary-in-the-Fields (usually called the *Kirk o' Field*).
Darnley was brought to lodge here on the 30th of January
1566–7. He had contracted the small-pox at Glasgow, and it was
thought necessary, or pretended to be thought necessary, to
lodge him in this place for air, as also to guard against infecting
the infant prince, his son, who was lodged in Holyroodhouse.
The house, which then belonged, by gift, to a creature of the Earl
of Bothwell, has been described as so very mean, as to excite
general surprise. Yet, speaking by comparison, it does not
appear to have been a bad temporary lodging for a person in
Darnley's circumstances. It consisted of two storeys, with a
turnpike or spiral staircase behind. The gable adjoined to the
town wall, which there ran in a line east and west, and the cellar

had a postern opening through that wall. In the upper floor were a chamber and closet, with a little gallery having a window also through the town wall. Here Darnley was deposited in an old purple travelling bed. Underneath his room was an apartment in which the queen slept for one of two nights before the murder took place. On the night of Sunday, February 9, she was attending upon her husband in his sick room, when the servants of the Earl of Bothwell deposited the powder in her room, immediately under the king's bed. The queen afterwards took her leave, in order to attend the wedding of two of her servants at the palace.

It appears, from the confessions of the wretches executed for this foul deed, that, as they returned from depositing the powder, they saw 'the Queenes grace gangand before thame with licht torches up the Black Frier Wynd'. On their returning to Bothwell's lodging at the palace, that nobleman prepared himself for the deed, by changing his gay suit of 'hose, stockit with black velvet, passemented with silver, and doublett of black satin of the same maner,' for 'ane uther pair of black hose, and ane canves doublet white, and tuke his syde [*long*] riding-cloak about him, of sad English claith, callit the new colour.' He then went, attended by Paris, the queen's servant, Powry, his own porter, Pate Wilson, and George Dalgliesh, 'downe the turnpike altogedder, and along the bak of the Queenes garden, till you come to the bak of the cunyie-house [*mint*], and the bak of the stabbillis, till you come to the Cannogate fornent the Abbey zett.' After passing up the Canongate, and gaining entry with some difficulty by the Netherbow Port, 'thai gaid up abone Bassentyne's hous on the south side of the gait, and knockit at ane door beneath the sword slippers, and callit for the laird of Ormistounes, and one within answerit he was not thair; and thai passit down a cloiss beneath the Frier Wynd [*apparently Todrig's Wynd*], and enterit in at the zett of the Black Friers, till thay came to the back wall and dyke of the town wall, whair my lord and Paris past in over the wall.' The explosion took place soon after, about two in the morning. The earl then came back to his attendants at this spot, and 'thai past all away togidder out at the Frier zett, and sinderit in the Cowgait.' It is here evident that the alley now called the High School Wynd was the avenue by which the conspirators approached the scene of their atrocity. Bothwell himself, with part of his attendants, went up the same wynd 'be east the frier wynd', and crossing the High Street, endeavoured to get out of the city by leaping a broken part of the town wall in Leith Wynd, but finding it too high, was obliged to rouse once more the porter at the Netherbow. They then passed – for every motion of the villains has a strange interest – down St Mary's Wynd, and along the south back of the Canongate, to the earl's lodgings in the palace.

The house itself, by this explosion, was destroyed, '*even,*' as the queen tells in a letter to her ambassador in France, '*to the very grund-stane.*' The bodies of the king and his servant were found next morning in a garden or field on the outside of the town wall.

The University of Edinburgh

[55] The original building in 1769; from *A Tour in Scotland MDCCLXIX* by Thomas Pennant.

The college is a mean building; it contains the houses of the Principal and a few of the Professors: the Principal's house is supposed to be on the site of that in which *Henry Darnly* was murdered, then belonging to the Provost of the *Kirk* of *field*. The students of the university are dispersed over the town, and are about six hundred in number; but wear no academic habit. The students are liable to be called before the Professors, who have power of rebuking or expelling them: I cannot learn that either is ever exerted; but, as they are for the most part volunteers for knowledge, few of them desert her standards. There are twenty-two Professors of different sciences, most of whom read lectures: all the chairs are very ably filled; those in particular which relate to the study of medicine, as is evident from the number of ingenious physicians, *élèves* of this university, who prove the abilities of their masters. The *Museum* had, for many years, been neglected; but, by the assiduity of the present Professor of natural history, bids fair to become a most instructive repository of the *naturalia* of these kingdoms.

[56] Laying the foundation stone of the new university on South Bridge (now the Old College), 1789; from *Memorials of His Time* by Lord Cockburn.

. . . In November 1789 we got a half holiday to see the foundation stone of the new college laid, which was done with great civic and masonic pomp. Forty years more did not see the edifice completed. Only those who knew the adjoining grounds at this time can understand how completely its position has been since destroyed. With the exception of a few paltry and easily removable houses on the west and north, the ground all round it was entirely open. Nicolson Street was partly, and College Street

The University (Old College), South Bridge; by Thomas Shepherd
from *Modern Athens* . . ., 1829. The Old College is built on the site of
Kirk o' Field

entirely, unbuilt; and the College was so perfectly free on its east
or front side, that I saw the ceremonies both of laying the
foundation stone, and of President Dundas's funeral in 1787,
from a window in the west wing of the Royal Infirmary. The
spaces now occupied by the various buildings pressing on the
College were then covered with grass fields of gardens. How
often did we stand to admire the blue and yellow beds of crocuses
rising through the clean earth, in the first days of spring, in the
garden of old Dr Monro (the second), whose house stood in a
small field entering from Nicolson Street, within less than a
hundred yards south of the College.

The New Town

[57] The origins of the New Town; from 'Proposals for carrying on certain Public Works in the City of Edinburgh'.

(These proposals were printed anonymously, but were probably by Sir Gilbert Elliott of Minto, who was influenced by George Drummond, then Lord Provost of the city for the third time.)

The healthfulness of its [*Edinburgh's*] situation, and its neighbourhood to the *Forth*, must no doubt be admitted as very favourable circumstances. But how greatly are these overbalanced by other disadvantages almost without number? Placed upon the ridge of a hill, it admits but of one good street, running from east to west; and even this is tolerably accessible only from one quarter. Lanes leading to the north and south, by reason of their steepness, narrowness, and dirtiness, can only be considered as so many unavoidable nusances. Confined by the small compass of the walls and the narrow limits of the royalty, which scarcely extends beyond the walls, the houses stand more crouded than in any other town in *Europe*, and are built to a height that is almost incredible. Hence necessarily follows a great want of free air, light, cleanliness, and every other comfortable accommodation. Hence also many families, sometimes no less than ten or a dozen, are obliged to live overhead of each other in the same building; where, to all the other inconveniences, is added that of a common stair, which is not other in effect than an upright street, constantly dark and dirty. It is owing to the same narrowness of situation, that the principal street is incumbered with the herb-market, the fruit-market, and several others; that the shambles are placed upon the side of the *North-Loch*, rendering what was originally an ornament to the town, a most insufferable nusance. No less observable is the great deficiency of public buildings. If the parliament-house, the churches, and a few hospitals, be excepted, what other have we to boast of? There is no exchange for our merchants; no safe repository for our public and private records; no place of meeting for our magistrates and town-council; none for the convention of our boroughs, which is intrusted with the inspection of trade. To these and such other reasons it must be imputed, that so few people of rank reside in this city; that it is rarely visited by strangers; and that so many local prejudices, and narrow notions, inconsistent with polished manners and growing wealth, are still so obstinately retained. To such reasons alone it must be imputed, that Edinburgh, which ought to have set the first example of industry and improvement, is the last of our trading cities that has shook off the unaccountable supineness which has so long and so fatally depressed the spirit of this nation. . . .

To enlarge and improve this city, to adorn it with public buildings, which may be a national benefit, and thereby to remove, at least in some degree, the inconveniences to which it has hitherto been liable, is the sole object of these proposals.

[58] The New Town at the end of the eighteenth century; from *Scotland Delineated* by Robert Heron.

(Robert Heron, 1764–1807, author, journalist and translator, was the son of a Kirkcudbrightshire weaver; his works include the earliest biography of Robert Burns.)

With regard to the buildings that have of late risen in this City with such incredible rapidity, we may venture to say, that, in regularity and magnificence, they are scarcely equalled, or at least not excelled, by any in Europe.

The communication between the north and south parts of the City, is facilitated by two noble bridges. The North Bridge, founded by Provost Drummond, in 1763, is a fine specimen of modern architecture. The South Bridge, which is as elegant, though less stupendous, was begun by Provost Hunter Blair, in 1785.

At the northern extremity of the two bridges, stands the Register Office, a vast pile of modern architecture, possessing that character of grandeur and stability, that strongly marks its fitness for the purpose to which it is applied. A marble statue of his present Majesty stands under the superb dome in the centre of this building. From this place, Prince's Street stretches almost a mile to the west, in a straight line. The houses of this street face the Old City, and are regular and uniform through its whole extent. Were the deformed marsh, and rugged declivity, which at present appear in front of this fine street, converted into a smooth meadow and sloping bank, it would contribute not a little to the beauty of its situation. At the head of the North Loch (as the morass is called) stands St Cuthbert's or the West Church, decorated with a handsome spire.

We ought not to omit mentioning the great earthen mound opposite to Hanover Street, composed of the earth from the foundations of the new buildings, and which now forms a broad and convenient passage between the Old and New City. The medium height of this mound is about eighty feet.

Near the centre of the east end of the New Town is St Andrew's Square, an assemblage of uniform and elegant buildings.

On the east side of this square is the Excise Office. This edifice is justly esteemed a fine model of correct design and exquisite workmanship.

From this square, George's Street extends to the west. On the north side of this street stands St Andrew's Church, adorned with a tall, and very handsome spire. Opposite to it is the Physicians Hall; and a little farther to the west, the New Assembly Rooms.

Queen's Street presents its front to the north, and is consequently exposed to cold piercing winds in the winter season. This inconvenience, however, is compensated by the beauty of its prospect, and the salubrity of the air. Though this be the most northerly, it is one of the noblest streets of the City.

When Charlotte Square, at the west end of George's Street, shall be completed, this City will certainly surpass, in regularity and magnificence, every other in Great Britain.

[59] The spreading of the New Town; from *Memorials of His Time* by Lord Cockburn.

It was about this time that the Earl of Moray's ground to the north of Charlotte Square began to be broken up for being built on. It was then an open field of as green turf as Scotland could boast of, with a few respectable trees on the flat, and thickly wooded on the bank along the Water of Leith. Moray Place and Ainslie Place stand there now. It was the beginning of a sad change, as we then felt. That well-kept and almost evergreen field was the most beautiful piece of ground in immediate connection with the town, and led the eye agreeably over to our distant northern scenery. How glorious the prospect, on a summer evening, from Queen Street! We had got into the habit of believing that the mere charm of the ground to us would keep it sacred, and were inclined to cling to our conviction even after we saw the foundations digging. We then thought with despair of our lost verdure, our banished peacefulness, our gorgeous sunsets. But it was unavoidable. We would never have got beyond the North Loch, if these feelings had been conclusive. But how can I forget the glory of that scene! on the still nights in which, with Rutherfurd and Richardson and Jeffrey, I have stood in Queen Street, or the opening at the north-west corner of Charlotte Square, and listened to the ceaseless rural corn-craiks, nestling happily in the dewy grass. It would be some consolation if the buildings were worthy of the situation; but the northern houses are turned the wrong way, and everything is sacrificed to the multiplication of feuing feet.

[60] The Disruption takes place at the General Assembly of 1843 in St Andrew's Church (now the Church of St Andrew and St George), George Street; from the *Journal of Henry Cockburn*, 1831–1854, Volume II.

(The Disruption, which split the Church of Scotland, occurred when 474 ministers out of about 1,200 seceded to form the Free Church, on the issue of the Church's liability to statute law and judgements of the civil courts.)

Dr Welsh, Professor of Church History in the University of Edinburgh, having been Moderator last year, began the proceeding by preaching a sermon before his Grace the

St Andrew's Church, George St where the Disruption, which split the
Church of Scotland, took place in 1843; by Thomas Shepherd from
Modern Athens . . ., 1829

Commissioner in the High Church, in which what was going to
happen was announced and defended. The Commissioner then
proceeded to St Andrew's Church, where the Assembly was to be
held. The streets, especially those near the place of meeting, were
filled, not so much with the boys who usually gaze at the annual
show, as by grave and well-dressed people of the middle rank.
According to custom, Welsh took the chair of the Assembly.
Their very first act ought to have been to constitute the Assembly
of this year by electing a new Moderator. But before this was
done, Welsh rose and announced that he and others who had
been returned as members held this not to be a free Assembly –
that, therefore, they declined to acknowledge it as a Court of the

Church – that they meant to leave the very place, and, as a consequence of this, to abandon the Establishment. In explanation of the grounds of this step he then read a full and clear protest. . . .

As soon as it was read, Dr Welsh handed the paper to the clerk, quitted the chair, and walked away. Instantly, what appeared to be the whole left side of the house rose to follow. Some applause broke from the spectators, but it checked itself in a moment. 193 members moved off, of whom about 123 were ministers, and about 70 elders. Among these were many upon whose figures the public eye had long been accustomed to rest in reverence. They all withdrew slowly and regularly amidst perfect silence, till that side of the house was nearly empty.

They were joined outside by a large body of adherents, among whom were about 300 clergymen. As soon as Welsh, who wore his Moderator's dress, appeared on the street, and people saw that principle had really triumphed over interest, he and his followers were received with the loudest acclamations. They walked in procession down Hanover Street to Canonmills, where they had secured an excellent hall, through an unbroken mass of cheering people, and beneath innumerable handkerchiefs waving from the windows. But amidst this exultation there was much sadness and many a tear, many a grave face and fearful thought; for no one could doubt that it was with sore hearts that these ministers left the Church, and no thinking man could look on the unexampled scene and behold that the temple was rent, without pain and sad forebodings. No spectacle since the Revolution reminded one so forcibly of the Covenanters. . . .

[61] The New Town, 1878, and Princes Street Gardens; from *Edinburgh, Picturesque Notes* by Robert Louis Stevenson.

It is as much a matter of course to decry the New Town as to exalt the Old; and the most celebrated authorities have picked out this quarter as the very emblem of what is condemnable in architecture. Much may be said, much indeed has been said, upon the text; but to the unsophisticated, who call anything pleasing if it only pleases them, the New Town of Edinburgh seems, in itself, not only gay and airy, but highly picturesque. An old skipper, invincibly ignorant of all theories of the sublime and beautiful, once propounded as his most radiant notion for Paradise: 'The New Town of Edinburgh, with the wind the matter of a point free.' He has now gone to that sphere where all good tars are promised pleasant weather in the song, and perhaps his thoughts fly somewhat higher. But there are bright and temperate days – with soft air coming from the inland hills, military music sounding bravely from the hollow of the gardens, the flags all waving on the palaces of Princes Street – when I have seen the town through a sort of glory, and shaken hands in sentiment with the old sailor. And indeed, for a man who has been much tumbled round Orcadian skerries, what scene could be more agreeable to witness? On such a day, the valley wears a surprising air of festival. It seems (I do not know how else to put my meaning) as if it were a trifle too good to be true. It is what Paris ought to be. It has the scenic quality that would best set off a life of unthinking, open-air diversion. It was meant by nature for the realization of the society of comic operas. And you can imagine, if the climate were but towardly, how all the world and his wife would flock into these gardens in the cool of the evening, to hear cheerful music, to sip pleasant drinks, to see the moon rise from behind Arthur's Seat and shine upon the spires and monuments and the green tree-tops, in the valley. Alas! and the next morning the rain is splashing on the window, and the passengers flee along Princes Street before the galloping squalls.

Fergusson, our Edinburgh poet, Burns's model, once saw a butterfly at the Town Cross; and the sight inspired him with a worthless little ode. This painted countryman, the dandy of the rose garden, looked far abroad in such a humming neighbourhood; and you can fancy what moral considerations a youthful poet would supply. But the incident, in a fanciful sort of way, is characteristic of the place. Into no other city does the sight of the country enter so far; if you do not meet a butterfly, you shall certainly catch a glimpse of far-away trees upon your walk; and the place is full of theatre tricks in the way of scenery. You peep under an arch, you descend stairs that look as if they would land you in a cellar, you turn to the back-window of a grimy tenement in a lane:– and behold! you are face-to-face with distant and bright prospects. You turn a corner, and there is the sun going down into the Highland hills. You look down an alley and see ships tacking for the Baltic.

[62] Walking in Princes Street, about 1814; from *Reminiscences* by Thomas Carlyle.

In my student days the chosen Promenade of Edinburgh was Princes Street; from the East end of it, to and fro, westward as far as Frederick Street, or farther if you wished to be less jostled, and have the pavement more to yourself: there, on a bright afternoon, in its highest bloom probably about 4–5 p.m., all that was brightest in Edinburgh seemed to have stept out to enjoy, in the fresh pure air, the finest city prospect in the World and the sight of one another, and was gaily streaming this way and that. From Castle Street or even the extreme west there was a visible increase of bright population, which thickened regularly east-ward, and in the sections near the Register Office or extreme east, had become fairly a lively crowd, dense as it could find stepping-ground, – never needed to be denser, or to become a crush, so many side-streets offering you free issue all along, and the possibity of returning by a circuit, instead of abruptly on your steps. The crowd was lively enough, brilliant, many-coloured, many-voiced, clever-looking (beautiful and graceful young womankind a conspicuous element); crowd altogether elegant, petite, and at its ease tho' on parade; something as if of unconsciously rhythmic in the movements of it, as if of harmonious in the sound of its cheerful voices, bass and treble, fringed with the light laughters: a quite pretty kind of natural concert and rhythms of march; into which, if at leisure, and carefully enough dressed (as some of us seldom were) you might introduce yourself, and flow for a turn or two with the general flood. It was finely convenient to a stranger in Edinburgh, intent to employ his eyes in instructive recreation; and see, or hope to see, so much of what was brightest and most distinguished in the place, on those easy terms. As for me, I never could afford to promenade or linger there; and only a few times, happened to float leisurely thro', on my way elsewhither. Which perhaps makes it look all the brighter now in far-off memory, being so *rare* as, in one sense, it surely is to me! Nothing of the same kind now [*1868*] remains in Edinburgh; already in 1832, you in vain sought and inquired where the general promenade, then, was? The general promenade was, and continues, nowhere – as so many infinitely nobler things already do!

[63] Walking in Princes Street, 1935; from *Scottish Journey* by Edwin Muir.

Princes Street in the evening is like a country platform where the train is late; there is the same intense and permitted scrutiny of one's fellow-passengers, the same growing expectation, and behind these the same sense, too, or rather a greater one, of wariness and prolonged disappointment. For the train never arrives at this platform, and so waiting becomes a thing with an existence of its own, which can no longer call up any definite image such as the arrival of a train, and is forced to find alleviation finally in distractions, in temporary liaisons with one's stranded companions. Perhaps in the background there persists a faith that a train will arrive some day, an unimaginable train such as the world has never seen before. But prolonged waiting breeds frustration and finally resignation; and a man gets used to his platform and finds it is after all a tolerable place, where he can take his pleasure as well as in any other. Until at last he grows weary of it, retires definitely, into matrimony perhaps, and leaves the field to passengers younger, more sanguine and more expectant than himself.

One of the advantages of this platform life is that it increases people's powers of observation, and of resistance to observation. In Princes Street you are seen, whoever you may be, and this knowledge, partly alarming and partly exhilarating like a plunge into cold water, forces the pedestrian to assemble his powers and be as intent as his neighbours. The concentrated force of observation sent out by the people he passes is sometimes so strong that he has the feeling of breaking, as he passes, through a series of invisible obstacles, of snapping a succession of threads laden with some retarding current. In London he can walk the most crowded streets for hours without feeling that he is either visible or existent: a disconcerting, almost frightening experience for a Scotsman until he gets used to it. But the crowd in a London street is mainly composed of people who are going somewhere, while the crowd in Princes Street is simply there; and even if you are going somewhere you cannot ignore it; it acquisitively stretches out and claims you. For it is there not only to observe, but also to be observed, and if you omit one of these duties you strike at its *amour-propre*, and perhaps at its existence. If a continuous relay of absent-minded philosophers could be let loose in Princes Street, the very foundations of its life would be shaken, and it would either rise and massacre these innocent revolutionaries or else die of disappointment.

[64] Princes Street in 1960; from *Edinburgh* by Eric Linklater.

Princes Street is a sort of schizophrenia in stone. On the one side, climbing with a ponderous grace against the southern sky, are verdurous slopes and a precipitous hill of naked rock, from which rise again the high walls of the Castle and a cluster of buildings, of no great beauty, but decently domesticated within ramparts decorated here and there with little pepperboxes of turrets, the mischievous reminders of desperate sallies and the bloody endurance of the valiant, starving men who sometime garrisoned the heights. Nothing could be finer than this aspect of a natural grandeur solemnized by memories of human pain and heroism; and to match it, or complement it, the northern side of the street should be the home of a rich and dignified commerce: of commerce in a long and graceful arcade whose columns marched to a measured but sprightly pace and whose windows

A view from the Castle, 1850, looking towards Princes Street, Princes
Street Gardens, and the Scott Monument, with Calton Hill in the
distance; by David Roberts and J.D. Harding

revealed an inner wealth by nicely ordered selection. This,
however, is not a description of Princes Street as a place of
business.

The north front of 'the Lang Gait' is a curious and disconcerting array of shops, stores, emporiums and bazaars without form
or order, pattern or design. Many of its shops are agreeable
enough – built to an ample and efficient plan, well lighted for a

display of merchandise. In the far east is the magnificent Register House, in the middle the massive dignity of the New Club. But the street as a whole – its north side, that is – is a creation of municipal anarchy, and its occasional resemblance to an oriental bazaar is truly startling. It is, of course, one of the charming ironies of history that whereas our mercantile fathers bought their way into the darkness of Africa with beads and bangles and cheap looking-glasses, we their offspring cannot set foot on that stirring continent without being pestered to buy beads and brooches and picture postcards. The traffic has become reciprocal, and that one must accept. But it is a pity, none the less, that some of the 'souvenirs' of Scotland exposed for sale in Princes Street would look equally at home in the boat of a native vendor in Port Said.

The street itself, the thoroughfare, has of late been vastly improved by removal of the rails and cables between which a rattling fleet of tram-cars used to ply on their Calvinistically predestined courses; and there are many who hope that before long the City Fathers will rid Princes Street Gardens of the railway lines that so incongruously intrude upon them. They are handsome gardens, but their flower-beds cannot be improved by the great gouts of smoke and volcanic fumes expelled from arrested locomotives. Here, where the railway runs immediately below the Rock, the ruffled waters of the Nor' Loch used to catch the light. At one time there were fish in the loch, but then, apparently, it grew foul with dead dogs and sewage, and the decision to drain it was no doubt a wise one.

The Mound

[65] The building of The Mound; from *The Beauties of Scotland* by Robert Forsyth (1805).

Another communication between the centre of the city and the New Town of Edinburgh has of late years been opened, by means of a mound of earth laid from the Lawn-market across the North Loch. This mound was made passable for carriages in three years. It is above 800 feet in length. On the north it is 58 feet in height, and on the south 92. The quantity of earth above the surface is 290,167 cubic yards: and from the nature of the soil, it is supposed to have sunk to such a degree, that there is now below ground half as much as appears above, or that, in other words, one-third of the whole mass is concealed from the view. Hence, as it stands at present, it amounts to 435,250 cubical yards of travelled earth; and if a cubical yard is held equal to three cartloads, it will be found that this mound contains 1,305,780 loads in all. Had the work been performed at the expence of four pence *per* cart, digging, filling, and carrying, which is very moderate, the amount is L.32,643,15s. In fact, however, it cost the community nearly nothing. It is said to have originated in the following manner. George Boyd, a shopkeeper in the Lawn-market, who sold tartan, was extremely fond of visiting the New Town to observe the progress of the buildings by which the capital of his native country was about to be so remarkably extended and adorned. Finding it inconvenient to go round by the North Bridge, he prevailed with his neighbours to join with him in contributing a small sum of money to defray the expence of laying stepping stones across the North Loch, which, though drained, was still as at present a sort of swamp or morass. He next persuaded some of the persons employed in erecting houses in the New Town to convey to the same spot their rubbish, and the earth dug out in laying the foundations of their buildings. A tolerable foot-path was thus made, which in the neighbourhood received the appellation of *Geordie Boyd's Brig*. The advantage derived from an undertaking of the same sort, upon a greater scale, was soon perceived. Permission was granted to the builders in the New Town to deposit in this spot the whole earth and rubbish which they had occasion to remove. This was accepted as a privilege, because no place was found so convenient for that purpose. The magistrates obtained the authority of parliament for removing certain houses in the Lawn-market, to open a communication with the Mound by a regular street; and before he died, the original projector of the work had the mortification to see his own shop pulled down for this purpose.

Calton Hill

[66] The view from Calton Hill, 1829; from *Modern Athens,
Displayed in a Series of Views of Edinburgh in the Nineteenth
Century* . . .

From the east end of Waterloo-place a flight of broad steps leads
to the foot-path which winds round the *Calton Hill*. In traversing
this, the spectator views in succession, the endless range of streets
which compose the New Town, bounded by the Corstorphine
Hills; – the Firth of Forth, with the distant mountains; – the
Town and Harbour of Leith; – Musselburgh Bay, terminated by
North Berwick Law; – Arthur's Seat, and Salisbury Craigs, with
Holyrood House in the plain beneath; – and lastly, the darkened
masses of the Old Town, skirted and guarded on one side by the
ancient Citadel.

[67] The view from Calton Hill, 1879; from *Edinburgh,
Picturesque Notes* by Robert Louis Stevenson.

On the north, the Calton Hill is neither so abrupt in itself nor has
it so exceptional an outlook; and yet even here it commands a
striking prospect. A gully separates it from the New Town. This
is Greenside, where witches were burned and tournaments held
in former days. Down that almost precipitous bank, Bothwell
launched his horse, and so first, as they say, attracted the bright
eyes of Mary. It is now tessellated with sheets and blankets out to
dry, and the sound of people beating carpets is rarely absent.
Beyond all this, the suburbs run out to Leith; Leith camps on the
seaside with her forest of masts; Leith roads are full of ships at
anchor; the sun picks out the white pharos upon Inchkeith
Island; the Firth extends on either hand from the Ferry to the
May; the towns of Fifeshire sit, each in its bank of blowing smoke,
along the opposite coast; and the hills inclose the view, except to
the farthest east, where the haze of the horizon rests upon the

open sea. There lies the road to Norway: a dear road for Sir
Patrick Spens and his Scots Lords; and yonder smoke on the
hither side of Largo Law is Aberdour, from whence they sailed to
seek a queen for Scotland.

> '*O lang, lang, may the ladies sit,*
>   *Wi' their fans into their hands,*
> *Or ere they see Sir Patrick Spens*
>   *Come sailing to the land!*'

These are the main features of the scene roughly sketched. How
they are all tilted by the inclination of the ground, how each
stands out in delicate relief against the rest, what manifold detail,
and play of sun and shadow, animate and accentuate the
picture, is a matter for a person on the spot, and turning swiftly
on his heels, to grasp and bind together in one comprehensive
look. It is the character of such a prospect, to be full of change
and of things moving. The multiplicity embarrasses the eye; and
the mind, among so much, suffers itself to grow absorbed with
single points. You remark a tree in a hedgerow, or follow a cart
along a country road. You turn to the city, and see children,
dwarfed by distance into pigmies, at play about suburban
doorsteps; you have a glimpse upon a thoroughfare where people
are densely moving; you note ridge after ridge of chimney-stacks
running downhill one behind another, and church spires rising
bravely from the sea of roofs. At one of the innumerable
windows, you watch a figure moving; on one of the multitude of
roofs, you watch clambering chimney-sweeps. The wind takes a
run and scatters the smoke; bells are heard, far and near, faint
and loud, to tell the hour; or perhaps a bird goes dipping evenly
over the housetops, like a gull across the waves. And here you are
in the meantime, on this pastoral hillside, among nibbling sheep
and looked upon by monumental buildings.

Return thither on some clear, dark, moonless night, with a
ring of frost in the air, and only a star or two set sparsely in the
vault of heaven; and you will find a sight as stimulating as the
hoariest summit of the Alps. The solitude seems perfect; the
patient astronomer, flat on his back under the Observatory

dome and spying heaven's secrets, is your only neighbour; and yet all round you there comes up the dull hum of the city, the tramp of countless people marching out of time, the rattle of carriages and the continuous keen jingle of the tramway bells. An hour or so before, the gas was turned on; lamp-lighters scoured the city; in every house, from kitchen to attic, the windows kindled and gleamed forth into the dusk. And so now, although the town lies blue and darkling on her hills, innumerable spots of the bright element shine far and near along the pavements and upon the high façades. Moving lights of the railway pass and repass below the stationary lights upon the bridge. Lights burn in the Jail. Lights burn high up in the tall *lands* and on the Castle turrets, they burn low down in Greenside or along the Park. They run out one beyond the other into the dark country. They walk in a procession down to Leith, and shine singly far along Leith Pier. Thus, the plan of the city and her suburbs is mapped out upon the ground of blackness, as when a child pricks a drawing full of pinholes and exposes it before a candle; not the darkest night of winter can conceal high station and fanciful design; every evening in the year she proceeds to illuminate herself in honour of her own beauty; and as if to complete the scheme – or rather as if some prodigal Pharaoh were beginning to extend to the adjacent sea and country – half-way over to Fife, there is an outpost of light upon Inchkeith, and far to seaward, yet another on the May.

[68]   The Nelson Monument and the National Monument in the 1880s; from *Old and New Edinburgh* by James Grant.

On the very apex of the hill [*Calton Hill*] stands the monument to Lord Viscount Nelson, an edifice in such doubtful taste that its demolition has been more than once advocated. Begun shortly after the battle of Trafalgar, it was not finished till 1816. A conspicuous object from every point of view, by sea or land, with all its defects it makes a magnificent termination to the vista along Princes Street. The base is a battlemented edifice, divided into small apartments and occupied as a restaurant. ... From

Calton Hill with the National and Nelson Monuments, seen from
Waterloo Place; by Thomas Shepherd from *Modern Athens . . .*, 1829

this pentangular base rises, to the height of more than 100 feet, a
circular tower, battlemented at the top, surmounted by a time-
ball and a flag-staff. . . .

A little to the north of it, on a flat portion of the hill, stand
twelve magnificent Grecian Doric columns, the fragment of the
projected national monument to the memory of all Scottish
soldiers and sailors who fell by land and sea in the long war with
France; and, with a splendour of design corresponding to the
grandeur of the object, it was meant to be a literal restoration of
the Parthenon at Athens. . . .

Notwithstanding the enthusiasm displayed when the undertaking was originated, and though a vast amount of money was
subscribed, the former subsided, and the western peristyle alone

was partially erected. In consequence of this remarkable end to an enterprise that was begun under the most favourable auspices, the national monument is often referred to as 'Scotland's pride and poverty'. The pillars are of gigantic proportions, formed of beautiful Craigleith stone; each block weighed from ten to fifteen tons, and each column as it stands, with the base and frieze, cost upward of £1,000. As a ruin it gives a classic aspect to the whole city. According to the original idea, part of the edifice was to be used as a Scottish Valhalla.

Arthur's Seat and Holyrood Park

[69] Ruins on Arthur's Seat; from *The Heart of Midlothian* by Walter Scott.

It was situated in the depth of the valley behind Salisbury Crags, which has for a background the north-western shoulder of the mountain called Arthur's Seat, on whose descent still remain the ruins of what was once a chapel, or hermitage, dedicated to Saint Anthony the Eremite. A better site for such a building could hardly have been selected; for the chapel, situated among the rude and pathless cliffs, lies in a desert, even in the immediate vicinity of a rich, populous, and tumultuous capital: and the hum of the city might mingle with the orisons of the recluses, conveying as little of worldly interest as if it had been the roar of the distant ocean. Beneath the steep ascent on which these ruins are still visible, was, and perhaps is still pointed out, the place where the wretch Nichol Muschat ... had closed a long scene of cruelty towards his unfortunate wife, by murdering her with circumstances of uncommon barbarity. The execration in which the man's crime was held extended itself to the place where it was perpetrated, which was marked by a small *cairn*, or heap of stones, composed of those which each chance passenger had thrown there in testimony of abhorrence, and on the principle, it would seem, of the ancient British malediction, 'May you have a cairn for your burial place!'

[70] Mutiny of the Seaforth Highlanders at Arthur's Seat; from *Kay's Edinburgh Portraits* . . .

This gentleman [*Captain M'Kenzie of Red Castle*] was an officer in Seaforth's regiment of Highlanders at the time of their revolt in 1778. The regiment had for some time been quartered in the Castle of Edinburgh; but, contrary to expectation, they were at length ordered to embark for Guernsey. Previous to this, a difference existed between the officers and men – the latter declaring that neither their bounty nor the arrears of their pay had been fully paid up, and that they had otherwise been ill-used. On the day appointed for embarkation (Tuesday, the 22nd September), the regiment marched for Leith; but farther than the Links the soldiers refused to move a single step. A scene of great confusion ensued; the officers endeavoured to soothe the men by promising to rectify every abuse. About five hundred were prevailed on to embark, but as many more were deaf to all entreaty; and, being in possession of powder and ball, any attempt to force them would have proved both ineffectual and dangerous. The mutineers then moved back to Arthur Seat, where they took up a position, and in which they continued encamped more than ten days. They were supplied plentifully with provisions by the inhabitants of Edinburgh, and were daily visited by crowds of people of all ranks. In the meantime, troops were brought into the city with the view of compelling the mutineers to submission, but no intimidation had any effect. General Skene Dunmore, and other noblemen and gentlemen, visited the mutineers; and, at last, after a great many messages had passed between the parties, a compromise was effected. The terms were – a pardon for past offences; all bye money and arrears to be paid before embarkation, and a special understanding that they should not be sent to the East Indies – a report having prevailed among the soldiers that they had been sold to the East India Company. So cautious were the mutineers, a bond had to be given confirming the agreement, signed by the Duke of Buccleuch, the Earl of Dunmore, Sir Adolphus Oughton, K.B., Commander-in-Chief, and General Skene, second in command in Scotland. After this arrangement, the Highlanders cheerfully proceeded to Leith and embarked.

[71] Dorothy Wordsworth climbs Arthur's Seat; from *Recollection of a Tour Made in Scotland AD 1803* by Dorothy Wordsworth.

Friday, September 6th. – The sky the evening before, as you may remember the ostler told us, had been 'gray and dull', and this morning it was downright dismal: very dark, and promising nothing but a wet day, and before breakfast was over the rain began, though not heavily. We set out upon our walk, and went through many streets to Holyrood House, and thence to the hill called Arthur's Seat, a high hill, very rocky at the top, and below covered with smooth turf, on which sheep were feeding. We climbed up till we came to St Anthony's Well and Chapel, as it is called, but it is more like a hermitage than a chapel – a small ruin, which from its situation is exceedingly interesting, though in itself not remarkable. We sate down on a stone not far from the chapel, overlooking a pastoral hollow as wild and solitary as any in the heart of the Highland mountains: there, instead of the roaring of torrents, we listened to the noises of the city, which were blended in one loud indistinct buzz, – a regular sound in the air, which in certain moods of feeling, and at certain times, might have a more tranquillizing effect upon the mind than those which we are accustomed to hear in such places. The castle rock looked exceedingly large through the misty air: a cloud of black smoke overhung the city, which combined with the rain and mist to conceal the shapes of the houses, – an obscurity which added much to the grandeur of the sound that proceeded from it. It was impossible to think of anything that was little or mean, the goings-on of trade, the strife of men, or every-day city business: – the impression was one, and it was visionary; like the conceptions of our childhood of Bagdad or Balsora when we have been reading the Arabian Nights' Entertainments. Though the rain was very heavy we remained upon the hill for some time, then returned by the same road by which we had come, through green flat fields, formerly the pleasure-grounds of Holyrood House, on the edge of which stands the old roofless chapel, of venerable architecture.

[72] Quarrying in Salisbury Crags; from *Memorials of His Time* by Lord Cockburn.

The year 1816 closed bitterly for the poor. There probably never were so many people destitute at one time in Edinburgh. The distress was less in severity than in 1797; but the population having increased, it was greater in extent. Some permanent good was obtained from the labour of the relieved. Bruntsfield Links were cleared of whins, and of old quarries; walks were made, for the first time, on the Calton Hill; and a path was cleared along the base of the perpendicular cliff of Salisbury Crags. Until then these two noble terraces were enjoyable only by the young and the active.

This walk along the Crags was the first thing that let the people see what we were in imminent danger of losing by the barbarous and wasteful demolition of the rock, which had been proceeding unchecked for nearly thirty years. When I first scrambled to that cliff, which must have been about 1788, the path along its base was certainly not six feet wide, and in some places there was no regular path at all. By 1816 the cliff had been so quarried away that what used to be the footpath was, in many places, at least 100 feet wide; and if this work had been allowed to go on for a few years more, the whole face of the rock would have disappeared. This would have implied the obliteration of some of the strata which all Edinburgh ought to have revered as Hutton's local evidence of the Theory of the Earth, and one of the most peculiar features of our scenery. The guilty would have been – first, the Hereditary *Keeper* of the Park, who made money of the devastation by selling the stones; secondly, the Town Council and the Road Trustees, who bought them; thirdly, the Crown and its local officers, who did not check the atrocity. Of these the Crown was the least criminal. It did interfere at last; and it was reserved for Henry Brougham, who had often clambered among these glorious rocks as a boy, to pronounce as Chancellor the judgment which finally saved a remnant of them.

[73] Queen Victoria's military reviews in Holyrood Park; from *Old and New Edinburgh* by James Grant.

A public event of great importance in this locality was the Royal Scottish Volunteer Review before the Queen on the 7th of August, 1860, when Edinburgh, usually so empty and dull in the dog days, presented a strange and wonderful scene. For a few

Queen Victoria's Review of Scottish Volunteers in Holyrood Park,
Edinburgh in 1881 – view from St Anthony's Chapel. 'Undeterred by
the incessant deluge of rain, the Queen remained till the last . . .' From
the *Illustrated London News*

days before this event regiments from all parts of Scotland came pouring into the city, and were cantoned in school-houses, hospitals, granaries, and wherever accommodation could be procured for them. The Breadalbane Highlanders, led by the white-bearded old marquis, attracted special attention, and, on the whole, the populace seemed most in favour of kilted corps, all such being greeted with especial approbation.

Along the north wall of the park there was erected a grand stand capable of containing 3,000 persons. The royal standard of Scotland – a splendid banner, twenty-five yards square – floated from the summit of Arthur's Seat, while a multitude of other standards and snow-white bell-tents covered all the inner slopes of the Craigs. By one o'clock all the regiments were in Edinburgh, and defiled into the park by four separate entrances at once, and were massed in contiguous close columns, formed into divisions and brigades of artillery, engineers, and infantry, the whole under the command of Lieutenant-General Sir G.A Wetherall, K.C.B.

The scene which burst upon the view of these volunteers as they entered the park, and the vast slopes of Arthur's Seat came in sight, will never be forgotten by those who were there, and made many a strong man's heart beat high and his eyes glisten. The vast hilly amphitheatre was crowded by more than 100,000 spectators, who made the welkin ring with their reiterated cheers, as the deep and solid columns, with all their arms glittering in the sun, were steadily forming on the grassy plain below. Every foot of ground upon the northern slopes not too steep for standing on was occupied, even to the summit, where the mighty yellow standard with the red lion floated out over all.

When the Queen, accompanied by the Prince Consort, the aged Duchess of Kent, and the royal children, came in front of the grand stand, the sight was magnificent, when more than two-and-twenty thousand rifles and many hundred sword-blades flashed out the royal salute, and then the arms were shouldered as she drove slowly along the line of massed columns. The ground was kept by the 13th Hussars, the 29th Regiment, 78th Highlanders (the recent heroes of Lucknow), and the West York Rifle Militia. The queen seemed in the highest spirits, wore a tartan dress, and bowed and smiled as the Volunteers passed the saluting point in quick time, to the number of 150 regiments, the Highland corps being played past by the pipers of the Ross-shire Buffs.

'So admirable was the arrangement', wrote one at the time, 'by which the respective corps were brought back to their original ground, that not ten minutes had elapsed after the marching-past of the last company before all was ready for the advance in line, the officers having taken post in review order, and the men standing with shouldered arms. On the signal being given, the whole line (of columns) advanced, the review bands playing. The effect of this was, in one word, indescribable, and when the whole was simultaneously halted, and the royal salute given, the silent grandeur of the scene, broken only by the National Anthem, sent a thrill of heart-stirring awe through the assembled multitude. But on a sudden the death-like silence is broken, and the pent-up enthusiasm of the Volunteers breaks forth like the bursting of some vast reservoir. A cheer, such as only Britons have in them to give, goes forth with the full power of 22,000 loyal throats – a cheer such as old Holyrood never heard before, caught up by the crowds on the hill, and rolled back to the plain, again and again to burst forth with redoubled energy, until it merges into one prolonged, heart-stirring, joyous roar – shakoes, caps and busbies, being held high on swords, rifles, and carbines; and then it was that the Queen spoke long to Sir George Wetherall, expressing her delight.' . . .

On the same ground, in August 1881, and before a vast multitude, Her Majesty reviewed a force of 40,000 Scottish Volunteers. So many men under arms had not been massed together in Scotland since James IV marched to Flodden. 'Although unhappily marred by continuous rain,' says the Duke of Cambridge's order, dated Edinburgh Castle, August 26th, 'the spectacle yesterday presented to her Majesty was an admirable sequel to the great review held recently at Windsor, and the Queen has observed with much gratification, the same soldierlike bearing, progress in discipline, and uniform good conduct, which distinguished the Volunteers there assembled, were conspicuous in a like degree on the present occasion. . . .

The Field Marshal Commander in Chief has been commanded by the Queen to express to the Volunteers of all ranks her entire satisfaction with the appearance of the troops assembled.'

The whole force was commanded by Major General Alastair Macdonald; and perhaps none were more applauded in the march past than the London Scottish, led by Lord Elcho. The bands of the Black Watch and 5th Fusileers were placed beside the saluting post, whereon was hoisted the royal standard, as borne in Scotland, the lion rampant being first and fourth in the quarterings.

Undeterred by the incessant deluge of rain, the Queen remained till the last, and so did the rest of the royal party; but even ere the second division had defiled before her the vast slopes of Arthur's Seat had been greatly denuded of spectators, 'and the great mass of umbrellas slipped down and gathered about the Holyrood gates, egress through which was still denied,' owing to certain instructions adapted evidently to a fair-weather gathering.

It was greatly to the credit of these Scottish troops, and a proof of their excellent discipline, that to the very close of that trying and harassing day, their behaviour was quiet, orderly, and admirable to the last, and not a single accident occurred.

The South Side

[74] George Square; from *Anecdotes and Egotisms* by Henry Mackenzie.

(Henry Mackenzie, 1745–1831, novelist and essayist, is looking back on the Edinburgh of his youth.)

The first Alison's Square, then Argyle Square, then Brown Square, and long after [*in 1766*] George Square. George Square one of the largest in Great Britain, if not the largest, with the exception of Lincoln's Inn Fields, if it can be called a Square. The south side of George Square at first left open, but Mr Brown asked £4,000 to allow it to continue so, a sum which the proprietors of the other sides would not give; so it was filled up by better houses than the north side and produced a large sum of feu duty to the proprietor. The new drain has been extremely beneficial to the houses of the Square, particularly on the south side, from which there is a beautiful prospect of Braid and Pentland Hills. This Square is well adapted for the residence of gentlemen whose estates are situated in the south of Scotland, and accordingly several do inhabit it; and indeed the houses are very good in themselves and supposed to be better and more substantially built than those of the New Town, where building became a trade, and profit was of course often more considered than convenience of substantial building.

[75] Skirmishes in George Square; from the General Preface to the Author's Edition of the Waverley Novels by Walter Scott.

The author's father, residing in George Square, in the southern side of Edinburgh, the boys belonging to that family, with others in the square, were arranged into a sort of company, to which a lady of distinction presented a handsome set of colours. Now this company or regiment, as a matter of course, was engaged in weekly warfare with the boys inhabiting the Crosscauseway, Bristo-street, the Potterrow, – in short, the neighbouring suburbs. These last were chiefly of the lower rank, but hardy loons, who threw stones to a hair's-breadth, and were very rugged antagonists at close quarters. The skirmish sometimes lasted for a whole evening, until one party or the other was victorious, when, if ours were successful, we drove the enemy to their quarters, and were usually chased back by the reinforcement of bigger lads who came to their assistance. If, on the contrary, we were pursued, as was often the case, into the precincts of our square, we were in our turn supported by our elder brothers, domestic servants, and similar auxiliaries.

[76] The eighteenth-century origins of the Royal Infirmary; from *The History of Edinburgh* by Hugo Arnot.

(The original Infirmary was built at the head of Robertson's Close, off the south-east end of the Cowgate. A second Royal Infirmary was built between 1738 and 1741 in what was then called Jamaica Street and is now called Infirmary Street, off the south-east corner of the South Bridge, and was opened in 1745. The third Infirmary, on the south side of Lauriston Place, was built between 1870 and 1879, and has been several times enlarged and expanded since then.)

The Royal Infirmary is undoubtedly the most noble of the institutions in Edinburgh reared by the hand of charity. Its purpose is to relieve the diseases of those who are oppressed by poverty.

In AD 1725, the Royal College of Physicians, who had long given advice and medicines *gratis* to the diseased and indigent, meditated the establishment of an institution, which the state of the poor in Edinburgh rendered so necessary. At that time, a fishing company was dissolved, and the partners were prevailed upon to assign part of their stock to promote this benevolent institution. A subscription, for this purpose, was, at the same

George Square, where the young Walter Scott indulged in street
skirmishes with local boys: his father's house is second from the left;
from James Grant's *Old and New Edinburgh*

time, urged; and application made by the General Assembly [*of
the Church of Scotland*], to recommend a subscription in all the
parishes within their jurisdiction. The Assembly most readily
granted their request, and sent copies of an act to that purpose to
the different incumbents. It met, however, with so little
obedience, that ten out of eleven of the whole established clergy
of Scotland utterly disregarded it. The sum of £2000 being,
notwithstanding, procured, the managers opened a small house
for reception of the sick poor on the 6th August 1729.

After the good effects of this institution, even when on a very limited scale, had been for some time experienced, the contributors towards it were, by royal charter of the 25th August 1736, erected into a body-corporate. After this charter was granted, the contributions increased to a considerable extent; so that the managers have been enabled from time to time to enlarge their scheme, and render it of more general utility. The benevolence and humanity of many individuals have afforded liberal subscriptions. The Earl of Hopetoun, in particular, during the early years of this institution, when its funds were slender, bestowed upon the Royal Infirmary an annuity of £400. In 1750, Dr Archibald Ker of Jamaica bequeathed to this corporation an estate in that Island of upwards of £200 Sterling a-year. In 1755, the Lords of the Treasury gave to the Infirmary £8000, which had been destined for support of the invalids; in consequence of which, the managers keep sixty beds constantly in readiness for the reception of sick soldiers. In this year, also, sick servants were begun to be admitted into the Infirmary, a ward having been fitted up for their reception.

But to none has the Royal Infirmary been more indebted than to George Drummond, Esq. who was seven [*actually, six*] times elected Lord Provost of Edinburgh. As the improvement of the city, and benefit of the community, were ever the objects which he assiduously endeavoured to promote; so this institution was, in a peculiar manner, the object of his public spirited exertions. The managers of the Infirmary have testified their sense of these obligations, by erecting, in their hall, a bust of him, executed by Nollekins, with this inscription, '*George Drummond, to whom this country is indebted for all the benefits which it derives from the Royal Infirmary.*'

[77] The Meadows in the late eighteenth century; from *Memorials of His Time*, by Lord Cockburn.

Except [*Professor John*] Robison, these men [*leaders of the 'Scottish Enlightenment', including William Robertson, Adam Ferguson, and Alexander Carlyle*] were all great peripatetics and the Meadows was their academic grove. There has never in my time been any single place in or near Edinburgh, which has so distinctly been the resort at once of our philosophy and our fashion. Under these trees walked, and talked and meditated, all our literary and scientific, and many of our legal, worthies. I knew little then of the grounds of their reputation, but saw their outsides with unquestioning and traditionary reverence; and we knew enough of them to make us fear that no such other race of men, so tried by time, such friends of each other and of learning, and all of such amiable manners and such spotless characters, could be expected soon to arise, and again ennoble Scotland.

[78] The Meadows in 1919; from *Two Worlds* by David Daiches.

A windy Spring day in Edinburgh, with bits of paper blown down the street and two small boys from Sciennes School kicking an empty tin can along the gutter. Across Melville Drive, in the Meadows, workmen are busy building stands and other wooden erections for the Highland Society's annual agricultural show, held in Edinburgh this year, though generally further north. The year is 1919, and I am six and a half years old. I am swinging on the heavy iron gate of our house in Millerfield Place, an exercise which gives me peculiar pleasure because we have only recently moved into the house and this variety of gate, though common in the city, is new to me. I am wearing a pair of dirty navy-blue shorts and a far from fresh brown jersey, and my uncombed hair is blowing about my face. My mother would be shocked indeed if she could see me now, but she is ill in a nursing home in Davidson's Mains (it has the enchanting name of Silverknowe, and I imagine it as a shining castle set beside the sea) and the aunt who has come up from London to look after my brother and sister and myself is out somewhere – with a young man, as my brother Lionel and I knowingly tell each other, though this is mere surmise: we are already precociously aware that my mother's younger sisters should be looking for husbands. As for my father, he is out at a meeting, or working in his study, or busy

Edinburgh Castle seen from the Meadows, about 1810: 'under these
trees walked, talked and meditated all our literary and scientific and . . .
legal worthies'; from James Grant's *Old and New Edinbugh*

trying to reconcile some dispute among different factions of his
congregation. We children are free to join in the rich street life of
the Edinburgh 'keelies'. The noise of the wind and the rattle of
the tin can sound like a tocsin of freedom in my ears. There is an
air of excitement in the afternoon.

I hear my name called: 'David! Where are you?' Lionel is
waving from the bottom of the street. 'Come on and watch the
workmen,' he calls. I hang on to the outside of the gate as it
swings round and clicks itself shut with the automatic device that

still fascinates me, then jump off and run down to meet him. We cross Melville Drive, climb over the iron railings that separate it from the Meadows (there are several open entrances, but we prefer to climb) and find ourselves amid heaps of stacked piles of wood. There are several children swarming around these, and we join them, clambering up and slipping down, chasing each other between the stacks, shouting at the top of our voices. Then one of the workmen, who are busy further down the field, sees us and shouts: 'Hey, get oot o' that!' We shout louder than ever, and the workman makes a threatening gesture. I find myself among a chorus of children chanting: 'Ha, ha, ha, ye canna catch me! Ha, ha, ha, ye canna catch me!' I am not happy about this defiance of the workmen, but I am encouraged by being a member of a group, and chant as loud as anyone. Then a shrill whistle blows, and the cry goes up: 'The parkie! The parkie!' and we all stream off towards the Middle Meadow Walk as the park-keeper, in his official uniform, whistles and waves at us.

[79] Sciennes Hill House – now part of a tenement block, it was the home of the philosopher and pioneer sociologist Adam Ferguson in the 1780s, and it was there that the boy Walter Scott met Robert Burns; from Scott's account of the meeting, quoted in the *The Life of Sir Walter Scott* by J.G. Lockhart.

As for Burns, I may truly say, *Virgilium vidi tantum*. I was a lad of fifteen in 1786–7, when he first came to Edinburgh, but had sense and feeling enough to be much interested in his poetry, and would have given the world to know him; but I had very little acquaintance with any literary people, and still less with the gentry of the west country, the two sets that he most frequented. Mr Thomas Grierson was at that time a clerk of my father's. He knew Burns, and promised to ask him to his lodgings to dinner, but had no opportunity to keep his word, otherwise I might have seen more of this distinguished man. As it was, I saw him one day at the late venerable Professor Fergusson's, where there were several gentlemen of literary reputation, among whom I remember the celebrated Mr Dugald Stewart. Of course we youngsters sate silent. The only thing I remember which was remarkable in Burns's manner, was the effect produced upon him by a print of Bunbury's, representing a soldier lying dead in the snow, his dog sitting in misery on one side, on the other his widow, with a child in her arms. These lines were written beneath –

> *Cold on Canadian hills, or Minden's plain,*
> *Perhaps that parent wept her soldier slain;*
> *Bent o'er her babe, her eye dissolved to dew,*
> *The big drops, mingling with the milk he drew,*
> *Gave the sad presage of his future years,*
> *The child of misery baptized in tears.*

Burns seemed much affected by the print, or rather the ideas which it suggested to his mind. He actually shed tears. He asked whose the lines were, and it chanced that nobody but myself remembered that they occur in a half-forgotten poem of Langhorne's, called by the unpromising title of 'The Justice of the Peace'. I whispered my information to a friend present, who mentioned it to Burns, who rewarded me with a look and a word, which, though of mere civility, I then received and still recollect with very great pleasure.

His person was strong and robust: his manners rustic, not clownish; a sort of dignified plainness and simplicity, which received part of its effect perhaps from one's knowledge of his extraordinary talents. ... There was a strong expression of strength and shrewdness in all his lineaments; the eye alone, I think, indicated the poetical character and temperament. It was large and of a dark cast, and glowed (I say literally *glowed*) when he spoke with feeling or interest. I never saw such another eye in a human head, though I have seen the most distinguished men in my time.

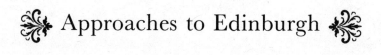

Approaches to Edinburgh

Leith

[80] The Earl of Hertford's army lands at Leith in 1544 and burns Edinburgh and Leith;from *The History of the Kirk of Scotland* by Mr David Calderwood.

(In 1544 Henry VIII, in an effort to persuade the reluctant Scots to let his son Edward marry the infant Mary Queen of Scots, resorted to what became known as the 'rough wooing', sending the Earl of Hertford to burn the city of Edinburgh.)

Upon the third of May, the yeere 1544, was seene a great navie of shippes in the Frith. .... The people flocked, some to the Castel-hill, some to the mountanes, and other eminent places, to gaze upon the shippes. But there was no care had of forces to resist, in cace of ane invasioun. Soone after six a clocke in the night, they cast anker in the raid [*road*] of Leith, moe than two hundred saile. Then the admirall, Sir Johne Dudley, Lord Lisle, shott a float boate, which sounded the depth frome Granton Hills till by east Leith, and so returned to her shippe. Men of judgement foresaw what it meant, but no credite was given to anie that would say, they minded to land; so everie man went to his rest, as if the shippes had been to guarde for their defense.

Upon the breake of day, the fourth of May, which was the Lord's day, they addressed themselves for landing, and ordered their shippes. The great shippes discharged their souldiours into smaller vessells; and these, by boats, sett upon the drie land, before tenne of the clocke, elleven thousand men, or moe. The governour and cardinall, seeing then the thing that they would not beleeve before, after they had bragged that they would fight, they fled als fast as horse could carie them, so that they approached not after within twentie myles of the danger. The Erle of Angus, his brother Sir George, the Master of Glencarne, and the Lord Maxwell, were sett that night at libertie, not for anie respect to the weele of the countrie, but least their friends and dependers sould joyne with the English against them; or to conciliat the favour of the people, which they had lost. Sir George said, merrilie, 'I thank King Henrie, and my gentle mastresse of England!' The English armie entered in Leith betwixt one and two of the clocke, found the tables covered, the dinners prepared, and abundance of wine and victuals, beside other substance. Upon Moonday came to them frome Berwick two thousand horsemen, or, as others write, foure thousand, under the conduct of Lord Williame Ivers, and his sonne, Sir Rawfe Ivers, to joyne with the armie at Leith. Upon Wednesday they marched towards Edinburgh; first spoiled, and then burnt the toun, and the palace of Halyrudhous. The horsemen took the castell of Craigmillar, where everie man sought to have saved his movables, it beeing the strongest hold neere the toun, except the castell of Edinburgh. But the laird raundered it without shott of hacquebutt, and, for this reward, was caused marche upon his feete to London. The English, seeing no resistance, hauled their canons up the High Street, by force of men, to the Butter-Trone, and above, and hazarded a shott against the fore entrie of the castell. But the wheele and axe-tree of one of the English cannons was brokin, and some of their men slaine, by a shott of ordinance out of the castell, so they left that rashe interprise. There were few houses, or village, burnt. Thereafter they spoiled and burnt Leith. When they had consumed both the touns, they loaded the shippes with the spoile, and both the armies departed at one time, the one by sea, and the other by land.

[81] The arrival of Mary Queen of Scots from France in 1561; from *The History of the Reformation in Scotland* by John Knox.

The nineteenth day of August, the year of God 1561, betwixt seven and eight hours before noon, arrived at Leith Marie, Queen of Scotland, then widow, with two galleys furth of France. In her company, besides her gentlewomen, called the Maries [*Mary Fleming, Mary Seton, Mary Beaton, and Mary Livingstone*], were her three uncles, Claude de Lorraine, the Duke d'Aumale, Francis de Lorraine, the Grand Prior, and

'A pretty little haven . . .' – a view of Leith in the County of Mid-Lothian; engraving by Paul Sandby *c.*1785

Rene de Lorraine, Marquis d'Elboeuf. There accompanied her also the Seigneur de Damville, son to the Constable of France, with other gentlemen of inferior condition, besides servants and officers.

The very face of heaven, the time of her arrival, did manifestly speak what comfort was brought into this country with her, to wit, dolour, darkness, and all impiety. In the memory of man, that day of the year, was never seen a more dolorous face of the heaven. Besides the surfeit [*immoderate*] wet, and corruption of the air, the mist was so thick and so dark, that scarce might any man espy another the length of two pair of butts. The sun was not seen to shine two days before, nor two days after. That forewarning gave God unto us; but, alas, the most part were blind!

At the sound of the cannons which the galleys shot, the multitude being advertised, happy were he and she that first might have the presence of the Queen! The Protestants were not the slowest, and therein they were not to be blamed. Because the Palace of Holyroodhouse was not thoroughly put in order – for her coming was more sudden than many looked for – she remained in Leith till towards evening, and then repaired thither.

[82] Leith in 1636; from *The Diary of Sir William Brereton.*

We went this morning to behold and take a view of Leith, where is the haven belonging to this city; which is a pretty little haven, neither furnished with near so many ships as it is capable of, nor indeed is it a large haven capable of many ships. There are two neat wooden piers here erected, which run up into the river, but not one ship saw I betwixt them. There are two churches in this town, which belongs unto and is subordinate to the city of Edenborough. This town of Leith is built all of stone, but it seemeth to be but a poor place, though seated upon a dainty haven: the country 'twixt this and Edenborough, and all hereabout this city, is corn, is situate betwixt the hills and the sea. Upon the top of the Toole-bowthe stands the head of Gawrie [*Gowrie*]. Here are pies (whereof I have had some this day to dinner) which are sold twelve for a penny English ... Many Highlanders we observed in this town in their plaids, many without doublets, and those who have doublets have a kind of loose flap garment hanging loose about their breech, their knees bare; they inure themselves to cold, hardship, and will not diswont themselves; proper, personable, well-complectioned men, and able men; the very gentlemen in their blue caps and plaids.

[83] Oyster-trading at Leith; from *The History of Edinburgh* by Hugo Arnot.

(Arnot, writing in 1779, gives the number of Leith ships engaged in foreign trade as fifty-two, and lists imports from and exports to Denmark, Norway, Russia, Prussia, Poland, Germany, Holland, France, Spain, Portugal, Guernsey, Ireland, Gibraltar, Italy, Sicily, North America and West Indies. £22,706 8s 5d was the amount of duty paid on wine imported at Leith in 1777.)

In the trade of Leith, the exportation of oysters deserves to be considered. This article began to be exported for the London market in the year 1773. From their beds in the Forth, they are taken to the Medway, and other rivers not distant from London, where they are deposited to fatten for the consumption of the great metropolis. But this trade is carried on with as much avidity for gain, as a profuse heir exerts in pursuit of pleasure; and both with a similar tendency, the destruction of the capital, which should afford them a continuance of their respective sources of pleasure. The quantity of oysters exported, has each year grown less, and the price has advanced proportionably. The first year, the oysters were sold at 4s per barrel. The price has risen gradually, and now mounts to 6s. In A.D. 1778, 8400 barrels were exported, which at 6s per barrel, amounts to £2520. Thus it appears, if the oyster-banks on the Forth are not dragged more sparingly, this commodity will be speedily exhausted.

[84] Leith and its commence in 1799; from *Scotland Delineated* by Robert Heron.

Leith is the sea-port of Edinburgh. It is a populous town, containing many handsome modern houses, though the ancient buildings are for most part neither elegant nor commodious. The town stands on both sides of the harbour, and is thus divided into South and North Leith. The harbour is formed by a noble stone pier, which was built about the beginning of the present century. At the end of the pier, a light-house, with reflecting lamps,

contributes considerably to the safety of shipping entering the
harbour. This harbour is now greatly improved, and accommodated with an elegant draw-bridge and a good quay. When the
proposed new bason and docks are added, this place will become
in every respect a safe, capacious and convenient station for
trading vessels. The road of Leith affords good anchoring ground
for ships of the greatest size. In 1781, a fleet of above five hundred
sail of merchant ships, under convoy of several ships of the line,
remained here for some weeks, and were supplied with fresh
provisions and vegetables from the Edinburgh market, without
any rise in the price of those articles. The commerce of this place
is very considerable. The vessels employed in the London trade,
called *Berwick Smacks*, have good accommodation for passengers.
The largest ships at this port, are those employed in the
Greenland whale-fishery, and in the trade to the West Indies.
The port of Leith is happily situated for the navigation of the
eastern seas. To Germany, Holland, and the Baltic, are
exported, lead, glass-ware, linen and woollen stuffs, and a
variety of other goods. From thence are imported, immense
quantities of timber, oak-bark, hides, linen rags, pearl-ashes,
flax, hemp, tar, and many other articles. From France, Spain
and Portugal; wines, brandy, oranges and lemons. From the
West Indies and America; rice, indigo, rum, sugar and logwood.
Ships of considerable size are built at this port, and several
extensive rope-works are here carried on. The flourishing
manufacture of bottle-glass, window-glass, and crystal, under
the direction of gentlemen possessed of great ingenuity and
opulence, well merits notice. Three glass-houses have long been
employed in this business, and three others have lately been
erected. A carpet-manufacture, a soap-work, and some iron-
forges, are also worthy of being mentioned.

[85] Leith's struggle for independence in the 1820s; from
Memorials of His Time by Lord Cockburn.

There was at this period, and for some years both before and
after, a very pretty quarrel between the people of Leith and the

town council of Edinburgh. The council was the proprietor of the harbour, and superior of the town of Leith; and, as such, had the entire mismanagement of that place. The result consequently was that the docks were bankrupt, and that though Leith was then even baser in its politics than its masters, the masters had scarcely a friend in that town. At last, after a long, and now incomprehensible, but most rancorous jumble which, whatever its details, was in principle a struggle for liberation on the one side, and for power on the other, Edinburgh fell into a pit dug by itself. It proposed to sell the harbour and the docks to a joint-stock company, which was to pay the debt, and to make money by imposing higher rates. The shares were speedily sold, and a bill to legalize the transaction was brought into Parliament. But the opposition to it was made irresistible by the discovery that several of the town council were share-holders; that is, that the public trustees had sold the subject of the trust to themselves for individual profit. After this truth had transpired, Abercromby had little difficulty in getting this municipal job quashed. The merchant company of Leith, a strongly Tory body, thanked him and their other parliamentary supporters – almost all Whigs, for 'defending the rights of an *unrepresented* trading port against the influence of a great city having powerful parliamentary friends'. The expression of this truth, that Leith had suffered from *want of representation*, was worth the whole struggle. The conflict raged for a long time: but its result was that, bit by bit, Leith was successful; till at last, though not a royal burgh, it, like some other places, was included in the general measures that were adopted in a few years after this for the cleansing of those chartered abominations. Throughout the course of the dispute, the parties were fairly enough matched in point of intemperance and unreasonableness; and if Leith had the advantage in coarse violence, Edinburgh was compensated by its superiority in disdainful insolence. In the eyes of quiet observers, the true value of the affair lay in its aiding the growth of independence in Leith. The town council actually succeeded in creating a public spirit in that prostrate place.

[86] King George IV lands at Leith in August 1822; from
The Life of Sir Walter Scott by J. G. Lockhart.

About noon on the 14th of August, the royal yacht and the
attendant vessels of war cast anchor in the Roads of Leith; but
although Scott's ballad-prologue had entreated the clergy to
'warstle for a sunny day', the weather was so unpropitious that it
was found necessary to defer the landing until the 15th. In the
midst of the rain, however, Sir Walter rowed off to the *Royal
George*; and, says the newspaper of the day –

'When his arrival alongside the yacht was announced to the
King, – "What!" exclaimed his Majesty, "Sir Walter Scott! The
man in Scotland I most wish to see! Let him come up." The
distinguished Baronet then ascended the ship, and was presented
to the King on the quarter-deck, where, after an appropriate
speech in name of the ladies of Edinburgh, he presented his
Majesty with a St Andrew's Cross in silver, which his fair subjects
had provided for him. The King, with evident marks of
satisfaction, made a gracious reply to Sir Walter, received the
gift in the most kind and condescending manner, and promised
to wear it in public, in token of acknowledgement to the fair
donors.'

To this record let me add, that, on receiving the poet on the
quarter-deck, his Majesty called for a bottle of Highland whisky,
and having drunk his health in this national liquor, desired a
glass to be filled for him. Sir Walter, after draining his own
bumper, made a request that the King would condescend to
bestow on him the glass out of which his Majesty had just drunk
his health; and this being granted, the precious vessel was
immediately wrapped up and carefully deposited in what he
conceived to be the safest part of his dress. [*On arriving home with
the glass in his coat, Scott found the poet George Crabbe awaiting him. Scott
entered, wet and hurried, and embraced Crabbe.*] The Royal gift was
forgotten – the ample skirt of the coat within which it had been
packed, and which he had hitherto held cautiously in front of his
person, slipped back to its more usual position – he sat down
beside Crabbe, and the glass was crushed to atoms. His scream

Sir Walter Scott, 1824; by Edwin Landseer

and gesture made his wife conclude that he had sat down on a pair of scissors, or the like; but very little harm had been done except the breaking of the glass, of which alone he had been thinking.

Newhaven

[87]   At Newhaven (the late fifteenth-century 'new haven' of James IV) was built and launched the *Great Michael*, said at the time to be the largest ship ever built; from *The History of Scotland from 1436 to 1565* by Robert Lindsay of Pittscottie.

(Robert Lindsay of Pittscottie, in Fife, c.1532–1580, was the first vernacular prose historian of Scotland.)

In this same year [*1511*] the king of Scotland bigged a great ship, called The Great Michael, which was the greatest ship, and of most strength, that ever sailed in England or France: for this ship was of so great stature, and took so much timber, that, except Falkland, she wasted all the woods in Fife, which was oak-wood, by all timber that was gotten out of Norway: For she was so strong, and of so great length and breadth (all the wrights of Scotland, yea, and many other strangers, were at her device, by the king's commandment; who wrought very busily in her; but it was year and day ere she was complete) to wit, she was twelvescore foot of length, and thirty-six foot within the sides. She was ten foot thick in the wall, outted jests of oak in her wall, and boards on every side, so stark and so thick, that no cannon could go through her. This great ship cumbered Scotland to get her to the sea. From that time that she was afloat, and her masts and sails complete, with tows and anchors effeiring thereto, she was counted to the king to be thirty thousand pounds of expences, by her artillery, which was very great and costly to the king, by all the rest of her orders; to wit, she bare many canons, six on every side, with three great bassils, two behind her dock, and one before, with three hundred shot of small artillery, that is to say, myand, and battert-falcon, and quarter-falcon, slings, pestilent serpetens, and double-dogs, with hagtor and culvering, cors-bows and hand-bows. She had three hundred mariners to sail her; she had sixscore of gunners, to use her artillery; and had a thousand men of war, by her captains, shippers and quarter-masters.

When this ship past to the sea, and was lying in the road the king gart shoot a cannon at her, to essay her if she was wight; but I heard say, it deared her not, and did her little skaith [*harm*]. And if any man believe that this description of the ship be not of verity, as we have written, let him pass to the gate of Tullibardin, and there, afore the same, ye will see the length and breadth of her, planted with hawthorn, by the wright that helped to make her. As for other properties of her, Sir Andrew Wood is my author, who was quarter-master of her; and Robert Bartyne, who was master-shipper.

[88] Newhaven fishwives; from *The Town and Port of Leith* by James Colston.

The Newhaven Fishwife's dress is quite unique. Compared with the women of other fisher communities, she is the yellow butterfly of her species. Her attire is more gaudy as a rule than of the fisherwomen of other districts. A writer in *Chamber's Edinburgh Journal* many years ago, thus describes it:– 'A cap of linen or cotton, surmounted by a stout napkin tied below the chin, composes the investiture of the hood; the showy structures wherewith other females are adorned being inadmissable from the broad belt which supports the creel, that is, fish-basket, crossing the forehead. A sort of woollen pea-jacket (usually of dark blue colour), with vast amplitude of skirt, conceals the upper part of the person, relieved at the throat by a liberal display of handkerchief. The under part of the figure is invested with a voluminous quantity of petticoat, of substantial material and gaudy colour, generally yellow, with stripes, so made as to admit a very free inspection of the ankle, and worn in such numbers that the bear mention of them would be enough to make a fine lady faint. One half of these ample garments is gathered over the haunches, puffing out the figure in an unusual and uncouth manner. White worsted stockings and stout shoes complete the picture. Imagine these investments endued upon a masculine but handsome form, notwithstanding the slight stoope forward, which is almost uniformly contracted – fancy the firm and elastic step, the toes slightly inclined inwards – and the ruddy complexion resulting from hard exercise, and you have the *beau idéal* of fishwives.' The Fisherwoman's garb has not escaped the notice and even patronage of the votaries of fashion. About fifteen years ago, it was all the rage in London and throughout the country generally. Young ladies donned the fisher lassie's costume, substituting silks for the more common and more durable material.

Craigcrook Castle

[89] Jeffrey and the Craigcrook gardens; from the *Life of Lord Jeffrey* by Lord Cockburn.

(Francis Jeffrey, 1773–1850, Scottish critic and jurist, was a founder of the *Edinburgh Review*, and a Judge of the Court of Session from 1834. Craigcrook Castle was considerably enlarged and modernized in the nineteenth century; it is still in private hands.)

[*Jeffrey*] had left Hatton in the autumn of 1814, and in the spring of 1815 transferred his rural deities to Craigcrook, where he passed all his future summers. It is on the eastern slope of Corstorphine Hill, about three miles to the north-west of Edinburgh. When he first became the tenant, the house was only an old *keep*, respectable from age, but inconvenient for a family; and the ground was merely a bad kitchen garden, of about an acre; all in paltry disorder. He immediately set about reforming. Some ill-placed walls were removed; while others, left for shelter, were in due time loaded with gorgeous ivy, and both protected and adorned the garden. A useful, though humble addition was made to the house. And, by the help of neatness, sense, evergreens, and flowers, it was soon converted into a sweet and comfortable retreat. The house received a more important addition many years afterwards; but it was sufficient without this for all that his family and his hospitalities at first required . . .

During the thirty-four seasons that he passed there, what a scene of happiness was that spot! To his own household it was all that their hearts desired. Mrs Jeffrey knew the genealogy, and the personal history and character, of every shrub and flower it contained. It was the favourite resort of his friends, who knew no such enjoyment as Jeffrey at that place. And, with the exception of Abbotsford [*Sir Walter Scott's country house*], there were more interesting strangers there than in any house in Scotland. Saturday, during the summer session of the courts, was always a day of festivity; chiefly, but by no means exclusively, for his friends at the bar, many of whom were under general invitations. Unlike some barbarous tribunals which feel no difference between the last and any other day of the week, but moil on with the same stupidity through them all, and would include Sunday if they could, our legal practitioners, like most of the other sons of bondage in Scotland, are liberated earlier on Saturday; and the Craigcrook party began to assemble about three, each taking to his own enjoyment. The bowling-green was sure to have its matches, in which the host joined with skill and keenness; the garden had its loiterers; the flowers, not forgetting the wall of glorious yellow roses, their worshippers; the hill its prospect seekers. The banquet that followed was generous; the wines never spared, but rather too various; mirth unrestrained, except by propriety; the talk always good, but never ambitious, and mere listeners in no disrepute. What can efface these days, or indeed any Craigcrook day, from the recollection of those who had the happiness of enjoying them?

Craigmillar Castle

[90] Queen Mary at Craigmillar; from *Old and New Edinburgh* by James Grant.

By far the most interesting associations of Craigmillar, like so many other castles in the south of Scotland, are those in which Queen Mary bears a part, as she made it a favourite country retreat. Within its walls was drawn up by Sir James Balfour, with unique legal solemnity, the bond of Darnley's murder, and there signed by so many nobles of the first rank who pledged themselves to stand by Bothwell with life and limb, in weal or woe, after its perpetration, which bond of blood the wily lawyer afterwards destroyed.

Some months after the murder of Rizzio, and while the grasping and avaricious statesmen of the day were watching the estrangement of Mary and her husband, on the 2nd December, 1560, Le Croc, the French Ambassador, wrote thus to the Archbishop of Glasgow:— 'The Queen is for the present at Craigmillar, about a league distant from this city. She is in the hands of the physicians, and I do assure you is not at all well, and do believe the principal part of her disease to consist in deep grief and sorrow. Nor does it seem possible to make her forget the same. Still she repeats these words – "I could wish to be dead!"'

The vicinity abounds with traditions of the hapless Mary. Her bed closet is still pointed out; and on the east side of the road, at Little France, a hamlet below the castle walls, wherein some of her French retinue was quartered, a gigantic plane – the largest in the Lothians – is to this day [*1883*] called 'Queen Mary's Tree,' from the unauthenticated tradition that her own hands planted it, and as such it has been visited by generations. In recent storms it was likely to suffer; and Mr Gilmour of Craigmillar, in September, 1881, after consulting the best authorities, had a portion of the upper branches sawn off to preserve the rest.

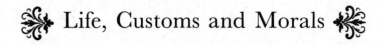 Life, Customs and Morals

[91] An English judgement of Scottish cleanliness in 1635; from *The Diary of Sir William Brereton.*

This city is placed in a dainty, healthful pure air, and doubtless were a most healthful place to live in, were not the inhabitants most sluttish, nasty, and slothful people. I could never pass through the hall, but I was constrained to hold my nose; their chambers, vessel, linen and meat, nothing neat, but very slovenly; only the nobler and better sort of them brave, well-bred men, and much reformed. This street, which may indeed deserve to denominate the whole city, is always full thronged with people, it being the market-place, and the only place where the gentlemen and merchants meet and walk, wherein they may walk dry under foot though there hath been abundance of rain. Some few coaches are here to be found for some of the great lords and ladies, and bishops. . . .

Their pewter, I am confident, is never scoured; they are afraid it should too much wear and consume thereby; only sometimes, and that but seldom, they do slightly rub them over with a filthy dish-clout, dipped in most sluttish greasy water. Their pewter pots, wherein they bring wine and water, are furred within, that it would loathe you to touch anything which comes out of them. Their linen is as sluttishly and slothfully washed by women's feet, who, after their linen is put into a great, broad, low tub of water, then (their clothes being tucked up above their knees) they step into the tub and tread it, and trample it with their feet (never vouchsafing a hand to nett [*clean*] or wash it withal) until it be sufficiently cleansed in their apprehensions and then it looks as nastily as ours doth when it is put unto and designed to the washing, as also it doth so strongly taste and smell of lant and other noisome savours, as that when I came to bed I was constrained to hold my nose and mouth together. To come into their kitchen, and to see them dress their meat, and to behold the sink (which is more offensive than any jakes) will be a sufficient supper, and will take off the edge of your stomach.

[92] 'Uncleanly customs' – early eighteenth century; from
Tour thro' the Whole Island of Great Britain by Daniel Defoe.

But, although I have made these Excuses for the Nastiness of this
Place, yet cannot the fact be denied. In a Morning, earlier than
seven o'Clock, before the human Excrements are swept away
from the doors, it stinks intolerably; for, after Ten at Night, you
run a great Risque, if you walk the Streets, of having Chamber-
pots of Ordure thrown upon your Head: and it sounds very oddly
in the Ears of a Stranger, to hear all Passers-by cry out, as loud as
to be heard to the uppermost Stories of the House, which are
generally six or seven high in the Front of the High street, *Hoad
yare Hoand*; that is, *Hold your Hand, and throw not, till I am passed.*

[93] 'Uncleanly customs' – late eighteenth century; from
Letters from Edinburgh ... by Captain Edward Topham.

This town has long been reproached with many uncleanly
customs. A gentleman, who lately published his travels through
Spain, says, that Madrid, some years ago, might 'have vied with
Edinburgh in filthiness'. It may probably be some pleasure to
this author, and to those who read him, to learn that his remarks
are now very erroneous.

But if a stranger may be allowed to complain, it would be, that
in these wynds, which are very numerous, the dirt is sometimes
suffered to remain two or three days without removal, and
becomes offensive to more senses than one. The magistrates, by
imposing fines and other punishments, have long put a stop to
the throwing any thing from the windows into the open street:
but as these allies are unlighted, narrow, and removed from
public view, they still continue these practices with impunity.
Many an elegant suit of clothes has been spoiled; many a
powdered, well-dressed maccaroni sent home for the evening:
and to conclude this period in Dr Johnson's own simple words,
'Many a full-flowing perriwig moistened into flaccidity.'

[94] A tavern meal in the eighteenth century; from *Letters from a Gentleman in the North of Scotland to his Friend in England* by Edward Burt.

(Edward Burt was employed by General Wade when he was building military roads in Scotland in the 1720s.)

Here I was told I might have a Breast of Mutton done upon the *Brander* (or Gridiron); but when it was brought me, it appeared to have been smoaked and dried in the Chimney Corner; and it looked like the glew that hangs up in an Ironmonger's Shop: This, you may believe, was very disgusting to the Eye; and for the Smell it had no other, that I could perceive, than that of the Butter wherewith it was greased in the Dressing; but, for my Relief, there were some new-laid Eggs which were my Regale: And now methinks I hear one of this Country say, – a true *Englishman*! He is already talking of Eating.

When I had been conducted to my Lodging-Room, I found the Curtains of my Bed were very foul by being handled by the dirty Wenches; and the old Man's Fingers being present with me, I sat down by the Fire, and asked myself, for which of my Sins I was sent into this Country; but I have been something reconciled to it since then, for we have here our Pleasures and Diversions, though not in such Plenty and Variety, as you have in *London*.

[95] A Welshman gives his impression of Edinburgh; from the novel *Humphry Clinker* (1771) by the Scottish novelist Tobias Smollett.

The beef and mutton are as delicate here as in Wales; the sea affords plenty of good fish; the bread is remarkably fine; and the water is excellent, though I'm afraid not in sufficient quantity to answer all the purposes of cleanliness and convenience; articles in which, it must be allowed, our fellow-subjects are a little defective – The water is brought in leaden pipes from a mountain in the neighbourhood, to a cistern on the Castle-hill, from whence it is distributed to public conduits in different parts of the city – From these it is carried in barrels, on the backs of male and female porters, up two, three,four, five, six, seven, and eight pairs of stairs, for the use of particular families – Every story is a complete house, occupied by a separate family; and the stair being common to them all, is generally left in a very filthy condition; a man must tread with great circumspection to get safe housed with unpolluted shoes – Nothing can form a stronger contrast, than the difference betwixt the outside and inside of the door; for the good-women of this metropolis are remarkably nice in the ornaments and propriety of their apartments, as if they were resolved to transfer the imputation from the individual to the public. You are no stranger to their method of discharging all their impurities from their windows, at a certain hour of the night, as the custom is in Spain, Portugal, and some parts of France and Italy – A practice to which I can by no means be reconciled; for notwithstanding all the care that is taken by their scavengers to remove this nuisance every morning by break of day, enough still remains to offend the eyes, as well as other organs of those whom use has not hardened against all delicacy of sensation.

The inhabitants seem insensible to these impressions, and are apt to imagine the disgust that we avow is little better than affectation; but they ought to have some compassion for strangers, who have not been used to this kind of sufferance; and consider, whether it may not be worth while to take some pains to vindicate themselves from the reproach that, on this account, they bear among their neighbours. As to the surprising height of their houses, it is absurd in many respects; but in one particular light I cannot view it without horror; that is, the dreadful situation of all the families above, in case the common staircase should be rendered impassable by a fire in the lower stories – In order to prevent the shocking consequences that must attend such an accident, it would be a right measure to open doors of communication from one house to another, on every story, by which the people might fly from such a terrible visitation.

[96] Dr Johnson in Edinburgh; from *Journal of a Tour to the Hebrides with Samuel Johnson LL.D.* by James Boswell.

On Saturday the fourteenth of August, 1773, late in the evening, I received a note from him, that he was arrived at Boyd's inn, at the head of the Canongate. I went to him directly. He embraced me cordially; and I exulted in the thought, that I now had him actually in Caledonia. Mr Scott's amiable manners, and attachment to our Socrates, at once united me to him. He told me that, before I came in, the Doctor had unluckily had a bad specimen of Scottish cleanliness. He then drank no fermented liquor. He asked to have his lemonade made sweeter; upon which the waiter, with his greasy fingers, lifted a lump of sugar, and put it into it. The Doctor, in indignation, threw it out of the window. Scott said, he was afraid he would have knocked the waiter down. Mr Johnson told me, that such another trick was played him at the house of a lady in Paris. He was to do me the honour to lodge under my roof. I regretted sincerely that I had not also a room for Mr Scott. Mr Johnson and I walked arm-in-arm up the High-street, to my house in James's court: it was a dusky night: I could not prevent his being assailed by the evening effluvia of Edinburgh. I heard a late baronet, of some distinction in the political world in the beginning of the present reign, observe, that 'walking the streets of Edinburgh at night was pretty perilous, and a good deal odoriferous'. The peril is much abated, by the care which the magistrates have taken to enforce the city laws against throwing foul water from the windows; but, from the structure of the houses in the old town, which consist of many stories, in each of which a different family lives, and there being no covered sewers, the odour still continues. A zealous Scotsman would have wished Mr Johnson to be without one of his five senses upon this occasion. As we marched slowly along, he grumbled in my ear, 'I smell you in the dark!' But he acknowledged that the breadth of the street, and the loftiness of the buildings on each side, made a noble appearance.

Dr Johnson and Boswell walking up the High Street – 'As we marched slowly along, he grumbled in my ear, "I smell you in the dark!"' From *The Picturesque Beauties of Boswell* by Thomas Rowlandson

[97] Adventures in an inn; from *Letters from Edinburgh* ... by Captain Edward Topham.

Since my last, which I delivered to your son, when I had the pleasure of seeing him in London, I have been a great traveller; and am now [*1774*] set down in Edinburgh for the winter season. I must confess I already shudder at the thoughts of this northern climate, and look with some apprehensions on the approach of cold weather; the severity of which, I doubt, the feebleness of my constitution will with difficulty be able to combat. However, I am in a tolerable comfortable habitation at present, and have fortunately procured an apartment somewhat elevated indeed, but commodious, and in a good situation. In a city so large as Edinburgh, the size of which you may easily conjecture from its being the metropolis of Scotland, I make no manner of doubt but you must be surprised to hear me consider myself as fortunate, in having found out a lodging, where I can sleep without molestation, and where I am neither poisoned by stench, or suffocated for want of air. A person like you, who has always been accustomed to meet with downy pillows, and splendid apartments, in the hotels of Paris and Lyons, can scarcely form in imagination the distress of a miserable stranger on his first entrance into this city: as there is no inn that is better than an alehouse, nor any accommodation that is decent, cleanly, or fit to receive a gentleman. On my first arrival, my companion and self, after the fatigue of a long day's journey, were landed at one of these stable-keepers (for they have modesty enough to give themselves no higher denomination) in a part of the town which is called the Pleasance [*at the eastern end of the Old Town*]; and on entering the house, we were conducted by a poor devil of a girl without shoes or stockings, and with only a single linsey-woolsey petticoat, which just reached half-way to her ankles, into a room where about twenty Scotch drovers had been regaling themselves with whisky and potatoes. You may guess our amazement, when we were informed, 'that this was the best inn in the metropolis – that we could have no beds, unless we had an inclination to sleep together, and in the same room with the company which a stage-coach had that moment dis-charged.' Well, said I to my friend (for you must know that I have more patience on these occasions than wit on any other) there is nothing like seeing men and manners, perhaps we may be able to repose ourselves at some coffee-house. Accordingly, on inquiry, we discovered that there was a good dame by the Cross, who acted in the double capacity of pouring out coffee, or letting lodgings to strangers, as we were. She was easily to be found out;

and with all the conciliating complaisance of a Maîtresse d'Hotel, conducted us to our destined apartments; which were indeed six stories high, but so infernal to appearance, that you would have thought yourself in the regions of Erebus.

The truth of this, I will venture say, you will make no scruple to believe, when I tell you, that in the whole we had only two windows, which looked into an alley five foot wide, where the houses were at least ten stories high, and the alley itself was so sombre in the brightest sunshine, that it was impossible to see any object distinctly. And now I am in the story-telling humour, I cannot omit giving you an account of an adventure which happened here very lately to a friend of mine; as it tallies in some measure with what I have already related, and serves to confirm the wretchedness of accommodation which must be put up with in this city. A gentleman from London, who had been appointed to some duty in a public office, came to Edinburgh, and having no friends to furnish him with a bed, and few acquaintance to give him any assistance, found himself obliged to conceal himself in one of these dark abodes, in order to be nigh the center of the town, where his employment compelled him to pass most part of the day. As he perceived his lodgings as good as his neighbours, it induced him to continue there, until he discovered himself extremely weak and emaciated, occasioned by constant violent perspirations in which he waked every morning. The observations, which some of his associates made on the alteration of his *embonpoint*, and the situation to which he was reduced (for from a stout and lusty man, he was now become a mere shadow) persuaded him to think himself really ill and in a consumption. Accordingly he sent for the professor, and another or two of the learned fraternity; who, with all the significancy of pompous physic, pronounced him to be in a very declining state, and administered every restorative which the Esculapian art could suggest or supply. But all without effect: he still continued to grow worse; and at length, almost totally exhausted, and giving himself a prey to despair, he sent up for his landlady to be a witness to his will; who, much concerned for the melancholy event, and with tears in her eyes, said, 'How unfortunate she had been since she kept house; that her two former lodgers had died with her; that she was sure she did every thing to serve them all; that, for her part, she always took care that their linen was well aired; and as for her rooms, nothing could be drier or more free from dampness; that her neighbour, good man, was a baker, and his oven was directly under them; that she was sure, therefore, they must be warm, and it was impossible to catch cold in her house.' – 'Good God,' cried the gentleman, 'an oven under my room! no wonder I am in a consumption after having been baked for these three months.' Upon which he sent for the baker, and found what she said was really true; that the oven was immediately under his bed, and that the decrease of his health had been in proportion to the increase of the baker's business. The discovery therefore being a much better medicine than any the professors could prescribe, he quitted this *enfer*, by degrees recovered his strength and constitution, and lives now to ridicule the oddity of the accident. After all this, I am sure you will agree with me, that 'tis extremely strange, that a city, which is a thoroughfare into all Scotland, and now little inferior in politeness to London in many respects, should not be better furnished with conveniencies for strangers, or have a public lodging-house where you can find tolerable entertainment. But it really has not: and I am the more surprised at it; as, in their manner of living, and many customs, I think the inhabitants much resemble the French. But in this particular what a difference between this place and Paris! where in a minute you may be provided with a house equal to one of the greatest nobility, with servants, equipage, and all the luxuries of elegance and taste; whilst at Edinburgh, without an inn to put your head into, and without a lodging that you can breathe in, you are obliged to blaze your stars to get any place to repose yourself, till better fortune, or better acquaintance, have interest enough to procure it you in some private house. – It is a pity – it is a disgrace to the country; and I should hope, ere long, the pride or good sense of Scotland will so far prevail, as to establish an Hotel in some suitable part of the town, to obviate the inconvenience of the want of these necessaries.

[98] Improvement in inns (1779); from *The History of Edinburgh* by Hugo Arnot.

There is no circumstance which contributes so much to impress strangers with a good opinion of the city of Edinburgh as the number and elegance of the hotels, and the excellence and cheapness of the taverns and eating-houses. Formerly it was a reproach to this metropolis, that the only houses for the reception of strangers were the public inns, which, as in London, were noisy, dirty, and incommodious. To avoid the inconvenience of these, when a person meant to reside for any time in town it was necessary to resort to private lodgings, in which, indeed, he might find quiet, and a decent accommodation, but could hardly expect either elegance or much convenience. Of late years there is, in these respects, a most remarkable change. There are a number of hotels in which strangers of any rank may find accommodation suited to their wishes; and that upon very reasonable terms. Several of these hotels, particularly those in the New Town, are not inferior in the variety and elegance of their apartments and furniture to the hotels of London. Besides these, private lodgings are to be had in every quarter of the city.

The inns, which are chiefly in the suburbs, are likewise greatly improved within these few years. The superior convenience and splendour of the hotels has stimulated the inn-keepers to a very laudable exertion in improving their houses in point of cleanliness, convenience, and readiness of service.

In London, where a great part of the community may be said to eat in public, (though not in the manner of the ancient Spartans), every street abounds in eating houses, cook's shops, chandler shops, and coffee houses, which are a species of tavern. In Edinburgh, the stile of manners is considerably different; and the man of business, the sober citizen, and industrious mechanic, find superior comfort in a domestic meal, to the tumultuous, and generally unsocial, table of an eating house. In this respect, however, a stranger is at no loss. Every hotel furnishes to its lodgers breakfast, dinner, and supper: And most of the coffee houses are likewise, in the stile of those of London eating houses, where, at the common hours of repast, a stranger is sure of finding well dressed victuals, and, in general, excellent wine. A stranger who lives in private lodgings, if he does not choose to board with the family, is supplied at an easy rate from these coffee houses, or from the taverns, with any thing that he requires for the table.

In no city of Europe are the markets of every kind better supplied than those of Edinburgh, nor are the prices to be at all complained of as immoderate. This will appear from the account that has been already given in the table of provisions in the preceding chapter, which exhibits to the eye both the great variety of all the articles of provision, and the prices at which they are sold. Accordingly, the tables of the citizens, or middling rank of people in Edinburgh, are more plentiful, and shew much greater variety than those of the same rank in London; and men of moderate fortune, choosing to reside in this metropolis, find that they can command luxuries of the table, which in London they would scarcely find within the reach of double the same income. This has been confessed by all strangers; and the proof of it is seen not only in the private tables of the inhabitants, but in the entertainments furnished in the taverns.

An Edinburgh tavern, (if a good one) is the best of all taverns. The custom of charging so much for every dish is not known in Scotland: The rule is, so much per head. It cannot fail to surprise an Englishman to see two complete courses, containing every thing nice in season, and frequently a desert of excellent fruits, at the rate of half-a-crown a head. But the great article from which the landlord expects his profit is the wine, which is there drank in much greater quantities than in England. . . .

In the capital taverns there are wines to be had of every kind, and of the best quality. The claret is in general excellent, and equal to any that is to be had in London. It has been remarked that the London claret is stronger than that which is commonly drank in Scotland. Its strength is not its own, but is given to it by the merchant, who knows the palate of those with whom he deals. But the Scotch claret is more genuine, and has a superior flavour, which recommends it to every person of taste. Of this some of the English connoisseurs have of late become sensible, and have commissioned their claret from Leith.

[99] High fashion in an oyster cellar; from *Letters from Edinburgh* ... by Captain Edward Topham.

You have so frequently run the round of all the fashionable diversions in other countries, as well as your own, and have so long imagined that gilded roofs and painted ceilings are the only scenes of festivity, that you will not easily believe there exists any other. There is, however, a species of entertainment, different indeed from yours, but which seems to give more real pleasure to the company who visit it, than either Ranelagh or the Pantheon. The votaries to this shrine of pleasure are numerous; and the manner is intirely new. As soon as the evening begins to grow late, a large party form themselves together, and march to the Temple; where, after descending a few steps for the benefit of being removed from profaner eyes, they are admitted by the good Guardian of it; who, doubtless, rejoices to see so large and well-disposed a company of worshippers. The Temple itself is very plain and humble. It knows no idle ornaments, no sculpture or painting; nor even so much as wax tapers – a few solitary candles of tallow cast a dim, religious light, very well adapted to the scene. There are many separate cells of different sizes, accommodated to the number of the religious, who attend in greater or smaller parties, as the spirit moves them. After the company have made the proper sacrifices, and staid as long as they think necessary, the utensils are removed, proper donations made to the priestess; who, like all others of her profession, is not very averse to money; and they retire in good order, and disperse for the evening.

In plain terms, this shrine of festivity is nothing more than an Oyster-cellar, and its Votaries the First People in Edinburgh. A few evenings ago I had the pleasure of being asked to one of these entertainments, by a Lady. At that time I was not acquainted with this scene of 'high life below stairs', and therefore, when she mentioned the word Oyster Cellar, I imagined I must have mistaken the place of invitation: she repeated it, however, and I found it was not my business to make objections; so agreed immediately. You will not think it very odd, that I should expect, from the place where the appointment was made, to have had a *partie tête–à-tête.* I thought I was bound in honour to keep it a secret, and waited with great impatience till the hour arrived. When the clock struck the hour fixed on, away I went, and enquired if the lady was there – 'O yes,' cried the woman, 'she has been here an hour, or more.' I had just time to curse my want of punctuality, when the door opened, and I had the pleasure of being ushered in, not to one lady, as I expected, but to a large and brilliant company of both sexes, most of whom I had the honour of being acquainted with.

The large table, round which they were seated, was covered with dishes full of oysters, and pots of porter. For a long time, I could not suppose that this was the only entertainment we were to have, and I sat waiting in expectation of a repast that was never to make its appearance. This I soon found verified, as the table was cleared, and glasses introduced. The ladies were now asked whether they would choose brandy or rum punch? I thought this question an odd one, but I was soon informed by the gentleman who sat next me, that no wine was sold here; but that punch was quite 'the thing'. The ladies, who always love what is best, fixed upon brandy punch, and a large bowl was immediately introduced. The conversation hitherto had been insipid, and at intervals: it now became general and lively. The women, who, to do them justice, are much more entertaining than their neighbours in England, discovered a great deal of vivacity and fondness for repartee. A thousand things were hazarded, and met with applause; to which the oddity of the scene gave propriety, and which could have been produced in no other place. The general ease, with which they conducted themselves, the innocent freedom of their manners, and their unaffected good-nature, all conspired to make us forget that we were regaling in a cellar; and was a convincing proof, that, let local customs operate as they may, a truly polite woman is every where the same. Bigotted as I know you to be to more fashionable amusements, you yourself would have confessed, that there was in this little assembly more real happiness and mirth, than in all the ceremonious and splendid meetings at Soho.

When the company were tired of conversation, they began to dance reels, their favourite dance, which they performed with great agility and perseverance. One of the gentlemen, however, fell down in the most active part of it, and lamed himself; so the dance was at an end for that evening. On looking at their watches, the ladies now found it was time to retire; the coaches were therefore called, and away they went, and with them all our mirth.

The company, which were now reduced to a party of gentlemen, began to grow very argumentative, and consequently very dull. Pipes and politics were introduced; but as I found we were not likely '*ex fumo dare lucem*', I took my hat, and wished them a good night. The bill for entertaining half a dozen very fashionable women, amounted only to two shillings a-piece. If you will not allow the entertainment an elegant one, you must at least confess that it is cheap.

[100] Music in St Cecilia's Hall in the 1770s; from *The History of Edinburgh* by Hugo Arnot.

The present Concert Hall, which is situated in a centrical part of the town, was built AD 1762. The plan was drawn by Mr Robert Mylne, architect of Blackfriars Bridge, after the model of the great Opera Theatre at Parma, but on a smaller scale; and the expence was defrayed by voluntary subscription among the members. The musical room is reckoned uncommonly elegant. It is of an oval form; the ceiling, a concave elliptical dome, lighted solely from the top by a lanthorn. Its construction is excellently adapted for music; and the seats ranged in the room in the form of an amphitheatre, besides leaving a large area in the middle of the room, are capable of containing a company of about five hundred persons. The orchestra is at the upper end, which is handsomely terminated by an elegant organ.

The bank consists of a *Maestro di capella*, an organist, two violins, two tenors, six or eight *ripienos*, a double, or *contra*-base, and harpsichord; and occasionally two French horns, besides kettle-drums, flutes, and clarinets. There is always one good singer, and there are sometimes two, upon the establishment. A few years ago, the celebrated Tenducci was at the head of this company. The principal foreign masters at present in the service of the musical society are, first violin, Signor Puppo; second, Signor Corri; violincello, Signor Schetky; singers, Signor and Signora Corri. All of these are excellent in their different departments. They have salaries from the society according to their respective merits.

Besides an extraordinary concert, in honour of St Cecilia, the patroness of music, there are usually performed, in the course of the year, two or three of Handel's oratorios. That great master gave this society the privilege of having full copies made for them, of all his manuscript oratorios. An occasional concert is sometimes given upon the death of a governor or director. This is conducted in the manner of a *concerto spirituale*. The pieces are of sacred music; the symphonies accompanied with the full organ, French horns, clarinets, and kettle-drums. Upon these occasions, the audience is in deep mourning, which, added to the pathetic solemnity of the music, has a noble and striking effect upon the mind.

The music generally performed, is a proper mixture of the modern and ancient stile. The former, although agreeable to the prevailing taste, is not allowed to debar the amusement of those, who find more pleasure in the old compositions. In every plan there are one or two pieces of Corelli, Handel, or Geminiani.

Among the number of members which is now increased to 200, there are many excellent performers, who take their parts in the orchestra, especially in extraordinary concerts, where sometimes a whole act is performed solely by the gentlemen-members.

Formerly some of the members of this society instituted a catch club, which met after the concert. On the great concert, in honour of St Cecilia, the governor and directors were in use to invite a few of their friends, and strangers of fashion, to an entertainment of this kind, after the concert, where select pieces of vocal music were performed, intermingled with Scots songs, duets, catches, and glees. There were many excellent voices in the catch club, who sung each their part at sight; and the easy cheerfulness which reigned in this select society, rendered their meetings delightful. When the Prince of Hesse was in Scotland in 1745–6, his Highness, and several of the nobility, were elegantly entertained by Lord Drummore, then governor of the musical society, and the gentlemen of the catch club. The prince was not only a *dillettante*, but a good performer on the violincello. The Scots songs, and English catches, were to him a new and an agreeable entertainment. The selection of company, which, for some years, gave high spirit and repute to this joyous convivial club, by degrees relaxed; it of course became numerous and expensive, and at last broke up.

Company are admitted to the entertainments of the concert, by special tickets, which are not transferable, and serve for the night only upon which they are granted; and, in the admission, which is always gratis, except at the benefit-concerts given for the emolument of performers, a preference is constantly shown to strangers. By an uniform adherence to the spirit and rules of the society, and a strict economy in the management of their funds, the musical society has subsisted these fifty years, with great honour and reputation; and, at present, it is esteemed one of the most elegant and genteel entertainments, conducted upon the most moderate expence, of any in Britain.

[101] St Cecilia's Hall in decline in the nineteenth century; from *Memorials of His Time* by Lord Cockburn.

It was the rise of the new town that obliterated our old peculiarities with the greatest rapidity and effect. It not only changed our scenes and habits of life, but, by the mere inundation of modern population, broke up and, as was then thought, vulgarised our prescriptive gentilities.

For example, Saint Cecilia's Hall was the only public resort of the musical, and besides being our most selectly fashionable place of amusement, was the best and the most beautiful concert room I have ever yet seen. And there have I myself seen most of our literary and fashionable gentlemen, predominating with their side curls, and frills, and ruffles, and silver buckles; and our stately matrons stiffened in hoops, and gorgeous satin; and our beauties with high-heeled shoes, powdered and pomatomed hair, and lofty and composite head dresses. All this was in the

Cowgate! the last retreat now-a-days of destitution and disease. The building still stands, though raised and changed, and is looked down upon from South Bridge, over the eastern side of the Cowgate Arch. When I last saw it, it seemed to be partly an old-clothesman's shop, and partly a brazier's. The abolition of this Cecilian temple, and the necessity of finding accommodation where they could, and of depending for patronage on the common boisterous public, of course extinguished the delicacies of the old artificial parterre. [*St Cecilia's Hall was restored and expanded by Edinburgh University in 1966.*]

[102] Scottish dancing: an English visitor's view; from *Letters from Edinburgh* ... by Captain Edward Topham.

I do not suppose any nation in Europe is more beautiful than the Scotch for a certain time; but the shape and symmetry of the boys, the complexion and features of the female sex, continue but a short period; as men, they are too coarse and ill-fashioned to be handsome; as women, too masculine and robust to be beauties. They dress their children in fancy-dresses, rather than any regular one; particularly the heads of the girls, which they ornament in the most unaffected pleasing manner possible, with ribbands and flowers: the habit of the boys also is elegant and plain: the performers, therefore, as to outside appearance, have every thing to recommend and set off their excellence in dancing.

But I cannot say, they are any great proficients in any style of dancing that requires grace: the Scotch are perfect strangers to it in any part of their life. Agility and strength are most natural to them, are their darling delight, which they endeavour to improve from their earliest infancy, and in which they arrive at much perfection. But as many people take the greatest pains to accomplish what they will never obtain; so the inhabitants of this country exhaust much time in learning a minuet, the most requisite part of which they never arrive at, namely, that elegant and graceful air which is the very essence of it, and of which the Italians and French are the only complete masters.

But if the Scotch are deprived of this advantage to their

persons, all-provident Nature has bestowed on them others, which are of much greater use to themselves and society. The want of grace is abundantly recompensed by a superiority of strength and manliness, and that sinewy arm, the very sight of which is sufficient to make a pampered offspring of the south stand amazed and tremble.

At these balls all the children dance minuets; which would be very tiresome and disagreeable, as well from the badness of the performance, as from the length of time they would take up, were they regularly continued. But the Dancing-masters enliven the entertainment by introducing between the minuets their High Dances, (which is a kind of Double Hornpipe) in the execution of which they excell perhaps the rest of the World. I wish I had it in my power to describe to you the variety of figures and steps they put into it. Besides all those common to the hornpipe, they have a number of their own, which I never before saw or heard of; and their neatness and quickness in the performance of them is incredible: so amazing is their agility, that an Irishman, who was standing by me the other night, could not help exclaiming in his surprise 'that by Jesus, he never saw children so *handy* with their *feet* in all his life.'

The motion of the feet is indeed the only thing that is considered in these dances, as they rather neglect than pay any attention to the other parts of the body; which is a great pity, since it would render the dance much more complete and agreeable, were the attitude of the hands and positions of the body more studied and understood by them. From the practice of these high dances one great advantage is derived to the young men, in giving prodigious powers to their ancles and legs; but I cannot say it is an ornamental advantage either to them or to the ladies; as it makes them too large in those parts for the proportion of the rest of the body, and takes off that fine tapering form which is so essential to real beauty.

I do not know any place in the world where dancing is made so necessary a part of polite education as in Edinburgh. For the number of inhabitants I suppose there are more Dancing-masters than in any other City; who gain large fortunes, though they instruct on very moderate terms, from the number of scholars who constantly attend them. In general they may be said to be very good ones, as well those of their own Country as Foreigners from most of the polite parts of Europe. Besides minuets and these high dances, they instruct the children in cotillons and allemandes, but not many of them, as they are sensible of their incapability of succeeding. In dancing, as in many other things, instruction and precept alone do not convey ideas so well as example and practice. Had they some few as excellent as Miss Lucinda B – to shew them what it was to move gracefully, elegantly, and unaffectedly, I do not doubt but that then they might make some progress, and reach some degree of perfection. I wish, therfore, for the benefit of this City, that you, and half a dozen of your female acquaintance, would pass the next winter in Edinburgh, in order to give them a model of a complete dancer.

[103] Ball-room discipline at the end of the eighteenth century; from *Memorials of His Time* by Lord Cockburn.

Our balls, and their manners, fared no better. The ancient dancing establishments in the Bow, and the Assembly Close, I know nothing about. Every thing of the kind was meant to be annihilated by the erection (about 1784) of the handsome apartments in George Street. Yet even against these, the new part of the old town made a gallant struggle, and in my youth the whole fashionable dancing, as indeed the fashionable every-thing, clung to George Square; where (in Buccleuch Place, close by the south-eastern corner of the square) most beautiful rooms were erected, which, for several years, threw the New Town piece of presumption entirely into the shade. And here were the last remains of the ball-room discipline of the preceding age. Martinet dowagers and venerable beaux acted as masters and mistresses of ceremonies, and made all the preliminary arrange-ments. No couple could dance unless each party was provided with a ticket prescribing the precise place, in the precise dance. If there was no ticket, the gentleman, or the lady, was dealt with as an intruder, and turned out of the dance. If the ticket had

Lord Henry Cockburn; by Sir Henry Raeburn

marked upon it – say for a country dance, the figures 3.5; this meant that the holder was to place himself in the 3d dance, and 5th from the top; and if he was anywhere else, he was set right, or excluded. And the partner's ticket must correspond. Woe on the poor girl who with ticket 2.7, was found opposite a youth marked 5.9! It was flirting without a license, and looked very ill, and would probably be reported by the ticket director of that dance to the mother. Of course parties, or parents, who wished to secure dancing for themselves or those they had charge of, provided themselves with correct and corresponding vouchers before the ball day arrived. This could only be accomplished through a director; and the election of a pope sometimes required less jobbing. When parties chose to take their chance, they might do so; but still, though only obtained in the room, the written permission was necessary; and such a thing as a compact to dance, by a couple without official authority, would have been an outrage that could scarcely be contemplated. Tea was sipped in side-rooms; and he was a careless beau who did not present his partner with an orange at the end of each dance; and the oranges and the tea, like everything else, were under exact and positive regulations. All this disappeared, and the very rooms were obliterated, as soon as the lately raised community secured its inevitable supremacy to the New Town. The aristocracy of a few predominating individuals and families came to an end; and the unreasonable old had nothing for it but to sigh over the recollection of the select and elegant parties of their youth, where indiscriminate public right was rejected, and its coarseness awed.

[104] 'Cawdies'; from *Letters from a Gentleman in the North of Scotland* ... by Edward Burt.

I then had no Knowledge of the *Cawdys*, a very useful Black-Guard, who attend the Coffee-Houses and publick Places to go of Errands; and though they are Wretches, that in Rags lye upon the Stairs, and in the Streets at Night, yet are they often considerably trusted, and, as I have been told, have seldom or never proved unfaithful.

These Boys know every body in the Town who is of any kind of Note, so that one of them would have been a ready Guide to the Place I wanted to find; and I afterwards wondered that one of them was not recommended to me by my new Landlady.

This Corps has a kind of Captain or Magistrate presiding over them, whom they call the Constable of the Cawdys, and in case of Neglect or other Misdemeanor he punishes the Delinquents, mostly by fines of Ale and Brandy, but sometimes corporally.

They have for the most Part an uncommon Acuteness, are very ready at proper Answers, and execute suddenly and well whatever Employment is assigned them.

Whether it be true or not I cannot say, but I have been told by several, That one of the Judges formerly abandoned two of his Sons for a Time to this Way of Life, as believing it would create in them a Sharpness which might be of Use to them in the future Course of their Lives.

[105] Or 'Cadies'?; from *Letters from Edinburgh* ... by Captain Edward Topham.

It is impossible at Edinburgh to be concealed or unknown: for though you enter into the City a mere traveller, and unacquainted, you cannot be there many hours before you are watched, and your name, and place of abode, found out by the Cadies. These are a Society of men who constantly attend the Cross in the High-street, and whose office it is to do any thing that any body can want, and discharge any kind of business. On this account it is necessary for them to make themselves acquainted with the residence and negotiation of all the inhabitants; and they are of great utility, as without them it would be very difficult to find any body, on account of the great height of the houses, and the number of families in every building. This Society is under particular regulations, and it requires some interest to become a member of it. It is numerous, and contains persons for every use and employment, who faithfully execute all commands at a very reasonable price. Whether you stand in need of a *valet de place*, a pimp, a thief-catcher, or a bully, your best resource is to the fraternity of

Cadies. In short, they are the tutelary guardians of the City; and it is intirely owing to them, that there are fewer robberies, and less house-breaking in Edinburgh, than any where else.

[106] Supper parties; from *Letters from Edinburgh* ... by Captain Edward Topham.

When dinners are given here, they are invitations of form. The entertainment of pleasure is their suppers, which resemble the *petit soupers* of France. Of these they are very fond; and it is a mark of their friendship to be admitted to be of the party. It is in these meetings that the pleasures of society and conversation reign, when the restraints of ceremony are banished, and you see people really as they are: and I must say, in honour of the Scotch, that I never met with a more agreeable people, with more pleasing or more insinuating manners, in my life. These little parties generally consist of about seven or eight persons, which prevents the conversation from being particular, and which it always must be in larger companies. During the supper, which continues some time, the Scotch Ladies drink more wine than an English woman could well bear; but the climate requires it, and probably in some measure it may enliven their natural vivacity. Without quoting foreign authorities, you will allow that a certain degree of wine adds great life to conversation. An English man, we know, is sometimes esteemed the best companion in the world after the second bottle; and who, before that, would not have opened his lips for the universe. After supper is removed, and they are tired of conversing, they vary the scene by singing, in which many of the Scotch excel. There is a plaintive simplicity in the generality of their songs, to which the words are extremely well adapted, and which, from the mouth of a pretty Scotch girl, is inconceivably attracting. You frequently feel the force of those very expressions, that at another time you would not understand, when they are sung by a young person whose inclinations and affections are frequently expressed in the terms made use of, and which the heart claims as its own. The eye, the whole countenance speak frequently as much as the voice; for I have sometimes found, that I had a very just idea of the tenor of a song, though I did not comprehend three words in the whole.

[107]　Changing meal times; from *The History of Edinburgh* by Hugo Arnot.

I shall now give a few facts respecting Edinburgh in the years 1763 and 1783, which have a more immediate connection with Manners.

In 1763 – People of fashion dined at two o'clock, or a little after; business was attended in the afternoon. It was common to lock the shops at one o'clock, and to open them after dinner at two.

In 1783 – People of fashion, and of the middle rank, dine at four and five o'clock: no business is done after dinner; that having of itself become a very serious business.

In 1763 – It was the fashion for gentlemen to attend the drawing-rooms of the ladies in the afternoons, to drink tea, and to mix in the society and conversation of women.

In 1783 – The drawing-rooms are totally deserted; and the only opportunity gentlemen have of being in ladies company, is when they happen to *mess* together at dinner or at supper; and even then an impatience is often shewn till the ladies retire. It would appear that the dignity of the female character, and the respect which it commanded, is considerably lessened, and that the bottle, and dissoluteness of manners, are heightened, in the estimation of the men.

[108]　Dinner hours and customs; from *Memorials of His Time* by Lord Cockburn.

The prevailing dinner hour [*in the late eighteenth century*] was about three o'clock. Two o'clock was quite common, if there was not company. Hence it was no great deviation from their usual custom for a family to dine on Sundays '*between sermons*' –that is between one and two. The hour, in time, but not without groans and predictions, became four, at which it stuck for several years. Then it got to five, which however was thought positively revolutionary; and four was long and gallantly adhered to by the haters of change as 'the good old hour'. At last even they obliged to give in. But they only yielded inch by inch, and made a desperate stand at half past four. Even five however triumphed, and continued the average polite hour from (I think) about 1806 or 1807 till about 1820. Six has at last prevailed, and half an hour later is not unusual.

The dinners themselves were much the same as at present. Any difference is in a more liberal adoption of the cookery of France. Ice, either for cooling or eating, was utterly unknown, except in a few houses of the highest class. There was far less drinking during dinner than now, and far more after it. The staple wines, even at ceremonious parties, were in general only port and sherry. Champagne was never seen. It only began to appear after France was opened by the peace of 1815. The exemption of Scotch claret from duty, which continued (I believe) till about 1780, made it till then the ordinary beverage. I have heard Henry Mackenzie and other old people say that, when a cargo of claret came to Leith, the common way of proclaiming its arrival was by sending a hogshead of it through the town on a cart, with a horn; and that anybody who wanted a sample, or a drink under pretence of a sample, had only to go to the cart with a jug, which, without much nicety about its size, was filled for a sixpence. The tax ended this mode of advertising; and, aided by the horror of everything French, drove claret from all tables below the richest.

Healths and toasts were special torments; oppressions which cannot now be conceived. Every glass during dinner required to be dedicated to the health of some one. It was thought sottish and rude to take wine without this – as if forsooth there was nobody present worth drinking with. I was present, about 1803, when the late Duke of Buccleuch took a glass of sherry by himself at the table of Charles Hope, then Lord Advocate; and this was noticed afterwards as a piece of Ducal contempt. And the person asked to take wine was not invited by any thing so slovenly as a look, combined with a putting of the hand upon the bottle, as is practised by near neighbours now. It was a much more serious affair. For one thing, the wine was very rarely on the table. It had to be called for; and in order to let the servant know to whom he was to carry it, the caller was obliged to specify his partner aloud. All this required some premeditation and courage. Hence timid men never ventured on so bold a step at all; but were glad to escape by only drinking when they were invited. As this ceremony was a mark of respect, the landlord, or any other person who thought himself the great man, was generally graciously pleased to perform it to every one present. But he and others were always at liberty to abridge the severity of the duty, by performing it by platoons. They took a brace, or two brace, of ladies or of gentlemen, or of both, and got them all engaged at once, and proclaiming to the sideboard – 'A glass of sherry for Miss Dundas, Mrs Murray, and Miss Hope, and a glass of port for Mr Hume, and one for me,' he slew them by coveys. And all the parties to the contract were bound to acknowledge each other distinctly. No nods, or grins, of indifference; but a direct look at the object, the audible uttering of the very words – 'Your good health,' accompanied by a respectful inclination of the head, a gentle attraction of the right hand towards the heart, and a gratified smile. And after all these detached pieces of attention during the feast were over, no sooner was the table cleared, and the after dinner glasses set down, than it became necessary for each person, following the landlord, to drink the health of every other person present, individually. Thus, where there were ten people, there were ninety healths drunk. This ceremony was often slurred over by the bashful, who were allowed merely to *look* the benediction; but usage compelled them to look it distinctly, and to each individual. To do this well, required some grace, and consequently it was best done by the polite ruffled and frilled gentlemen of the olden time.

This prandial nuisance was horrible. But it was nothing to what followed. For after dinner, and before the ladies retired, there generally began what were called '*Rounds*' of toasts; when each gentleman named an absent lady, and each lady an absent gentleman, separately; or one person was required to give an absent lady, and another person was required to match a gentleman with that lady, and the pair named were toasted, generally with allusions and jokes about the fitness of the union. And, worst of all, there were 'Sentiments'. These were short epigrammatic sentences, expressive of moral feelings and virtues, and were thought refined and elegant productions. A faint conception of their nauseousness may be formed from the following examples, every one of which I have heard given a thousand times, and which indeed I only recollect from their being favourites. The glasses being filled, a person was asked for his, or for her, sentiment, when this or something similar was committed – 'May the pleasures of the evening bear the reflections of the morning.' Or, 'May the friends of our youth be the companions of our old age.' Or, 'Delicate pleasures to susceptible minds.' 'May the honest heart never feel distress.' 'May the hand of charity wipe the tear from the eye of sorrow.' 'May never worse be among us.' There were stores of similar reflections; and for all kinds of parties, from the elegant and romantic, to the political, the municipal, the ecclesiastic, and the drunken.

[109] Edinburgh society in 1811; from *Autobiography* by Mrs Eliza Fletcher, 1770–1858.

(Mrs Fletcher was the wife of Archibald Fletcher, reformer and advocate.)

The society of Edinburgh at that time was delightful. The men then most distinguished in social intercourse, alike by literary reputation and amiable manners in society, were Walter Scott, Mr Jeffrey, Dr Thomas Brown, Mr MacKenzie, Mr Thomas Thomson, Professor Playfair, Mr Pillans, the Rev. Dr Alison, and Dr R. Morehead. A little before this time the forms of social meetings had somewhat changed from what they were when I knew Edinburgh first. Large dinner parties were less frequent, and supper parties – I mean hot suppers – were generally discarded. In their place came evening parties (sometimes larger than the rooms could conveniently hold) where card-playing generally gave place to music or conversation. The company met at nine, and parted at twelve o'clock. Tea and coffee were handed about at nine, and the guests sat down to some light cold refreshments later on in the evening; people did not in these parties meet to eat, but to talk and listen. There you would see a group (chiefly of ladies) listening to the brilliant talk of Mr Jeffrey; in a different part of the room, perhaps another circle, amongst whom were pale-faced reverential-looking students, lending their ears to the playful imaginative discussions of Dr Brown while Professor Playfair would sometimes throw in an ingenious or quiet remark, that gave fresh animation to the discourse. On other occasions, old Mr Mackenzie would enliven the conversation with anecdotes of men and manners gone by. It was this winter that Mrs Apreece and Mrs Waddington divided the admiration of the Edinburgh circles between them – the one attractive by the vivacity of her conversation, the other by her remarkable beauty and the grace of her manners.

[110] Reflections on the morning after; from *Memoirs and Correspondence of Mrs Grant of Laggan.*

(Mrs Grant was the wife of a minister who spent some time in the parish of Laggan, Inverness-shire (where she wrote *Letters from the Mountains* (1806) but lived in Edinburgh from 1810 until her death in 1838.)

I have this morning [*20 November 1811*] the muddiest head you can suppose, having had a party of friends with me on the last two evenings. To understand the cause of all this hospitality, you must know that, being a very methodical and economical family, every cow of ours, as we express it in our rustic Highland dialect, has a calf; that is to say, when we have a party, which in Edinburgh includes a cold collation, we are obliged to provide *quantum sufficit* for our guests, who, being of a description more given to good talking than good eating, are content to admire and be admired, and have little time to attend to vulgar gratifications; of consequence, the more material food, after contributing, like the guests, to embellish the entertainment, remains little diminished. As our wide acquaintance includes the greatest variety of people imaginable, there are among them a number of good, kind people, that dress finely, laugh heartily, and sing merrily, and have, in some instances, genealogy besides; yet on these good people the lions and lionesses of literature would think their roaring very ill bestowed. These, however, make a greater noise in their own way, and before their superior prowess the substantials soon vanish: they are in every sense less fastidious, happier because less wise, and more benevolent because less witty. An assemblage of these contented beings, who can amply appreciate the value of a custard, a jelly, or a jest on its second appearance, are convenient successors to the refined pretenders to originality, who prefer what is new to what is true, and would not for the world be caught eating blanc-mange while Mr Jeffrey and Dr Thomas Brown are brandishing wit and philosophy in each other's faces with electric speed and brilliance. These good fat people, who sing and eat like canary-birds, come with alacrity the day after, and esteem themselves too happy to be admitted so soon to consume mere mortal aliment in the very apartment where the delicacies of intellect were so lately shared among superior intelligences.

[111] Keeping the King's Birthday in 1665; from the *Intelligencer*, 1 June 1665, reprinted in Hugo Arnot's *The History of Edinburgh*.

Edinburgh, May 29, 1665, being his Majesty's [*Charles II*] birth and restauration day, was most solemnly kept by people of all ranks in this city. My Lord Commissioner, in his state, accompanied with his life-guard on horseback, and Sir Andrew Ramsay, Lord Provost of Edinburgh, Bailies, and Council, in their robes, accompanied with all the trained bands in arms, went to church, and heard the Bishop of Edinburgh, upon a text as fit as well apply'd for the work of the day. Thereafter, thirty-five aged men, in blue gowns, each having got thirty-five shillings in a purse, came up from the abbey to the great church, praying all along for his Majesty. Sermon being ended, his Grace entertained all the nobles and gentlemen with a magnificent feast, and open table. After dinner, the Lord Provost and council went to the cross of Edinburgh, where was planted a green arbour, loaded with oranges and lemons, wine liberally running for divers hours at eight several conduits, *to the great solace of the indigent commons there.* Having drunk all the royal healths, which were seconded by the great guns from the Castle, sound of trumpets and drums, vollies from the trained bands, and joyful acclamations from the people, they plentifully entertained the multitude. After which, my Lord Commissioner, Provost, and Bailies, went up to the Castle, where they were entertained with all sorts of wine and sweet-meats; and returning, the Lord Provost countenancing all the neighbours of the city that had put up bonefires, by appearing at their fires, being in great numbers; which jovialness continued with ringing of bells, and shooting of great guns till twelve o'clock at night.

[112] Keeping the King's Birthday in 1773; from the *Weekly Magazine or Edinburgh Amusement*, 10 June 1773.

Friday last, being the anniversary of his majesty's [*George III*] birth-day, when he entered into the 36th year of his age, was observed here with the greatest demonstrations of joy. In the morning the flag was displayed from the castle, at noon there was a round of the great guns, returned by three vollies from a party of the military drawn up on the Castle-hill, and accompanied by the ringing of the music-bells. About four in the afternoon, the lord provost, magistrates and council, attended by a number of noblemen and gentlemen, specially invited, with the officers of the army and trained-bands, assembled in the Parliament-house, where they drank the health of the day, and a variety of loyal toasts, announced by the flourish of trumpets, and vollies of small arms from the city-guard, drawn up in the Parliament close. After which the evening concluded with a brilliant assembly. – It is, however, to be regretted, that, on such days of festivity, the lower class of people seldom indulge their mirth without mischief. On this occasion they became, towards the evening, perfectly licentious, and, after their ammunition of squibs and crackers was exhausted, they employed dead cats, mud &c. which they discharged very plentifully on the city guard; and, when threatened to be chastised or apprehended, they betook themselves to the more dangerous weapons of stones and brickbats, &c. In this encounter several of the guard were wounded, and they in return dealt their blows pretty liberally, by which, amid the confusion, some innocent persons suffered along with the guilty. A number of young lads, suspected of having been concerned in the riot, were apprehended; but most of them were set at liberty next morning, by their friends becoming bail for their appearance when called. Five of the most active were committed to the tolbooth, upon application of the procurator fiscal, and still remain there where they will have time to repent of their folly in cool blood.

[113] Keeping King George III's birthday at the end of the eighteenth century; from *Memorials of His Time* by Lord Cockburn.

Another [*test of loyalty*] was *keeping* the King's birth-day. This day was the 4th of June, which for the 60 years that the reign of George the III. lasted gave an annual holiday to the British people, and was so associated in their habits with the idea of its being a free day, that they thought they had a right to it even after his Majesty was dead. And the established way of keeping it in Edinburgh was, by the lower orders and the boys having a long day of idleness and fire-works, and by the upper classes going to the Parliament House, and drinking the royal health in the evening, at the expense of the city funds. The magistrates who conducted the banquet, which began about seven, invited about 1500 people. Tables, but no seats except one at each end, were set along the Outer House. These tables, and the doors and walls, were adorned by flowers and branches, the trampling and bruising of which increased the general filth. There was no silence, no order, no decency. The loyal toasts were let off, in all quarters, according to the pleasure of the Town Councillor who presided over the section, without any orations by the Provost, who, seated in his robes, on a high chair, was supposed to control the chaos. Respectable people, considering it all an odious penance, and going merely in order to shew that they were not Jacobins, came away after having pretended to drink one necessary cup to the health of the reigning monarch. But all sorts who were worthy of the occasion and enjoyed it, persevered to a late hour, roaring, drinking, toasting, and quarrelling. They made the Court stink for a week with the wreck and the fumes of that hot and scandalous night. It was not unusual at old Scotch feasts for the guests, after drinking a toast, to toss their glasses over their heads, in order that they might never be debased by any other sentiment. The very loyal on this occasion availed themselves of this privilege freely, so that fragments of glass crunched beneath the feet of the walkers. The infernal din was aggravated by volleys of musketry, fired very awkwardly by the Town Guard, amidst the shouts of the mob, in the Parliament Close. The rabble, smitten by the enthusiasm of the day, were accustomed, and permitted, to think license their right, and exercised their brutality without stint. Those who were aware of what might take place on the street, retired from the banquet before the spirit of mischief was fully up. Those who came out so late as ten or even nine of the evening, if observed and unprotected, were fortunate if they escaped rough usage, especially if they escaped being '*Burghered*', or made to '*Ride the Stang*', a painful and dangerous operation, and therefore a great favourite with the mob. I forget when this abominable festival was given up. Not, I believe, till the poverty, rather than the will, of the Town Council was obliged to consent.

[114]   Tartan pageantry at George IV's visit to Edinburgh in 1822; from *The Life of Sir Walter Scott* by J. G. Lockhart.

(The cult of the tartan began with Sir Walter Scott's stage-managing King George IV's visit to Scotland; after that it developed rapidly, especially after Queen Victoria acquired

Balmoral Castle in 1852 and began to visit Scotland regularly. Scott was determined to present the Highland chiefs in their traditional kilted glory, and to have as many other Scots as possible (and also, on one occasion, the King himself) arrayed in tartan. This was his way of showing that George IV was now everywhere recognized as the legitimate successor to the old Stewart kings of Scotland.)

Whether all the arrangements which Sir Walter dictated or enforced, were conceived in the most accurate taste, is a different question. It appeared to be very generally thought, when the first programmes were issued, that the Highlanders, their kilts, and their bagpipes, were to occupy a great deal too much space in every scene of public ceremony connected with the King's reception. With all respect and admiration for the noble and generous qualities which our countrymen of the Highland clans have so often exhibited, it was difficult to forget that they had always constituted a small, and almost always an unimportant part of the Scottish population; and when one reflected how miserably their numbers had of late years been reduced in consequence of the selfish and hard-hearted policy of their landlords, it almost seemed as if there was a cruel mockery in giving so much prominence to their pretensions. But there could be no question that they were picturesque – and their enthusiasm was too sincere not to be catching; so that by-and-by even the coolest-headed Sassenach felt his heart, like John of Argyle's, 'warm to the tartan'. . . .

But Sir Walter had as many parts to play as ever tasked the Protean genius of his friend Mathews; and he played them all with as much cordial energy as animated the exertions of any Henchman or Piper in his company. His severest duties, however, were those of stage-manager, and under these I sincerely believe any other human being's temper and patience would very soon have given way. The local magistrates, bewildered and perplexed with the rush of novelty, threw themselves on him for advice and direction about the merest trifles; and he had to arrange everything, from the ordering of a procession to the cut of a button and the embroidering of a cross. Ere the greenroom in Castle Street [*Scott's Edinburgh house*] had dismissed provosts and baillies, and deacon-conveners of the trades of Edinburgh, it was sure to be besieged by swelling chieftains, who could not agree on the relative positions their clans had occupied at Bannockburn, which they considered as constituting the authentic precedent for determining their own places, each at the head of his own little theatrical *tail*, in the line of the King's escort between the Pier of Leith and the Canongate. It required all of Scott's unwearied good-humour, and imperturbable power of face, to hear in becoming gravity the sputtering controversies of such fiery rivals, each regarding himself as a true potentate, the representative of Princes as ancient as Bourbon; and no man could have coaxed them into decent co-operation, except him whom all the Highlanders, from the haughtiest MacIvor to the slyest Callum-Beg, agreed in looking up to as the great restorer and blazoner of their traditionary glories. He had, however, in all this most delicate part of his administration an admirable assistant in one who had also, by the direction of his literary talents, acquired no mean share of authority among the Celts – namely, the late General David Stewart of Garth, author of the *History of the Highland Regiments*. On Garth (seamed all over with the scars of Egypt and Spain) devolved the Toy-Captainship of the *Celtic Club*, already alluded to as an association of young civilians enthusiastic for the promotion of the philabeg [*kilt*] – and he drilled and conducted that motley array in such style, that they formed, perhaps, the most splendid feature in this plaided panorama. . . .

By six o'clock next morning, Sir Walter, arrayed in the 'Garb of old Gaul' (which he had of the Campbell tartan, in memory of one of his great-grandmothers), was attending a muster of these gallant Celts in the Queen Street Gardens, where he had the honour of presenting them with a set of colours, and delivered a suitable exhortation, crowned with their rapturous applause. Some members of the Club, all of course in their full costume, were invited to breakfast with him.

[115] Cries of Edinburgh; from *Anecdotes and Egotisms* by
Henry Mackenzie (who is looking back in the late 1820s).

Some of the old cries are now out of use. The cry of *Caller Laverocks*
was always heard in severe winters, when, in very deep snow, the
larks used to frequent in myriads the grounds in the neighbourhood of Newhaven and Laverockband, which last-mentioned
place got its name from that circumstance; but now all the
ground in that quarter being occupied by villas, the larks have
left it, changing the place for their emigration, as I have been
told, to the neighbourhood of the Solway firth, where the snow
does not lie. The lark was never much used for the table in
Scotland, tho' at the time to which I allude people whose
scruples against eating the poor songsters did not prevent them,
bought the larks from the women who sold them, generally the
wives of Newhaven fishers, at a season when the fishers made but
few excursions in the way of their trade. The laverocks were
certainly at that season good eating, I presume from the
circumstance of the frost preventing their feeding on bad fare.
There was a joke on a dinner given by Mrs Siddons, who was
accused of narrowness, that one course was chiefly composed of
larks. I believe the trade was given up some time ago [*February
1826*] to the great satisfaction of the lovers of the songs of these
birds.

There was a summer cry which had a good deal of music in it,
Curds and Green Whey, and another a little earlier in the season,
Wall Cresses, which was also bawled with a musical cadence.
When a boy I remember another cry brought here by an
Englishman, of which the poetry was set to music:

Wha'll buy my rare sausages?
  They're round,
  They're very sound,
They're nothing but fourpence the pound.

This might have been made into a catch like the *Yellow Sand* and
Banbury Ale, [but] catches are now out of fashion.

[116] The Scottish Enlightenment; from *Literary and Characteristical Lives of Gregory, Kames, Hume and Smith* by William Smellie.

(William Smellie was an Edinburgh printer, naturalist and antiquary, who printed and contributed to the first edition of the *Encyclopaedia Britannica* in 1771. He was a friend of most of the Edinburgh literati of the latter part of the eighteenth century.)

Mr Amyat, King's Chymist, a most sensible and agreeable English gentleman, resided in Edinburgh for a year or two. He one day surprised me with a curious remark. There is not a city in Europe, said he, that enjoys such a singular and such a noble privilege. I asked, What is that privilege? He replied, Here I stand at what is called the *Cross of Edinburgh*, and can, in a few minutes, take fifty men of genius and learning by the hand. The fact is well known; but to a native of that city, who has all his days been familiarized with it, and who has not travelled in other countries, that circumstance, though very remarkable, passes unnoticed: Upon strangers, however, it makes a deep impression. In London, in Paris, and other large cities of Europe, though they contain many literary men, the access to them is difficult; and, even after that is obtained, the conversation is, for some time, shy and constrained. In Edinburgh, the access of men of parts is not only easy, but their conversation and the communication of their knowledge are at once imparted to intelligent strangers with the utmost liberality. The philosophers of Scotland have no nostrums. They tell what they know, and deliver their sentiments without disguise or reserve. This generous feature was conspicuous in the character of Mr Hume. He insulted no man, but, when the conversation turned upon particular subjects whether moral or religious, he expressed his genuine sentiments with freedom, with force, and with a dignity which did honour to human nature.

[117] Bookselling in Edinburgh; from *Letters from Edinburgh* ... by Captain Edward Topham.

The most profitable trade now in Edinburgh appears to be that of a Bookseller. Of all the other advantageous branches this place has only received a part in conjunction with many other towns in Scotland; but they have appropriated this business at present entirely to themselves. If I am well informed, many thousand volumes are annually printed in this place, and sold in London or elsewhere. The cheapness of labour here, when compared with London, induces many Scotch Booksellers who reside there, to have their books printed at Edinburgh, and then sent to them; which they find much better than printing at their own shops: and for this purpose, many of them have partners in this place.

Some years ago the Printing-office at Glasgow was a formidable rival to that at Edinburgh; and had the two celebrated Printers there pursued their business, they might have carried away the whole trade of Scotland to themselves. But, alas! 'Men are but men,' as Tristram Shandy observes, 'and the best have their weaknesses.' An unfortunate desire seized these two gentlemen of instituting an academy of painting, and of buying a collection of pictures; forgetting that the place where this academy was to be instituted was amongst a society of tradesmen, who would throw away no money on such subjects. With this idea they bought paintings which nobody else will buy again, and which now lie upon their hands in high preservation. During the rage of this fancy, they forgot their former business, and neglected an art which, from their editions of Homer and Milton, might have made them immortal, to run after paltry copies of good paintings, which they had been informed were originals.

When I visited these gentlemen I had heard of their Printing, but never of their Academy. It was in vain that I asked for books; I had always a picture thrust into my hand; and like Boniface, though they had nothing in print worth notice, they said they could shew me a delicate engraving. You may well imagine that this ambition has prevented their former success: for though Poetry and Painting may be sister arts I never heard that

Painting and Printing were of the same family; if they are, their interests have been very opposite.

Banished from Glasgow this trade has settled at Edinburgh, and by the ingenuity and application of those who are engaged in it, has been brought to great perfection. I mean that perfection which includes every requisite in a book for the smallest price possible.

[118] Constable and the *Edinburgh Review* (founded in 1802); from *Memorials of His Time* by Lord Cockburn.

On looking back at those times [*the decades before 1802*], it is impossible not to be struck with the apparent absence of enlightened public views and capacities all over the community. I do not recollect a single Scotch work of any permanent, or almost of any respectable temporary, value, which even the excitement of that age produced. When the Edinburgh Review appeared it received no published opposition, and no material aid on public questions, from any person at that time in public life. Even at the bar, which had always contained the best educated and the ablest of the middle and upper ranks, and been in advance of all other classes, Horner, Brougham, or Jeffrey, at the age of twenty-five, or perhaps of twenty-one, were better prepared to instruct and direct the public than all the other counsel, either Whig or Tory, in practice when they came forward. Indeed the suppression of independent talent or ambition was the tendency of the times. Every Tory principle being absorbed in the horror of innovation, and that party casting all its cares upon Henry Dundas, no one could, without renouncing all his hopes, commit the treason of dreaming an independent thought. There was little genuine attraction for real talent, knowledge, or eloquence on that side; because these qualities can seldom exist in combination with abject submission. And indeed there was not much attraction for them among the senior and dominant Whigs, among whom there was a corresponding loyalty to the Earl of Lauderdale. The adherents of both parties were saved the trouble of qualifying themselves for taking any charge of public matters; the one by knowing that, in so far as their aid implied any independence, it would be offensive, and that, if they would only obey, their champion would be sure to carry them through; the other by despair of being either allowed to co-operate, or able to resist.

To Archibald Constable, the publisher of the Edinburgh Review, the literature of Scotland has been more indebted than to any other bookseller. Till he appeared, our publishing trade was at nearly the lowest ebb; partly because there was neither population nor independence to produce or to require a vigorous publisher; and partly, because the publishers we had were too spiritless even for their position. Our principal booksellers were Bell and Bradfure, and Manners and Miller, in the Parliament Close; Elphinstone Balfour, Peter Hill, and William Creech in the High Street; and William Laing in the Canongate. Laing was a good collector of good books, chiefly old ones, but did not publish much. Creech was connected with the publication of the works of Robertson and other respectable authors. All the rest were unimportant. Constable began as a lad in Hill's shop, and had hardly set up for himself when he reached the summit of his business. He rushed out, and took possession of the open field, as if he had been aware from the first of the existence of the latent spirits, which a skilful conjurer might call from the depths of the population to the service of literature. Abandoning the old timid and grudging system, he stood out as the general patron and payer of all promising publications, and confounded not merely his rivals in trade, but his very authors, by his unheard-of-prices. Ten, even twenty, guineas a sheet for a review, £2000 or £3000 for a single poem, and £1000 each for two philosophical dissertations, drew authors from dens where they would otherwise have starved, and made Edinburgh a literary mart, famous with strangers, and the pride of its own citizens.

[119] The first year of the Edinburgh International Festival, 1947; from *Edinburgh* by Eric Linklater.

It was a hungry year, a year of meagre rations, and in July the infinitesimal weekly allowance of meat was again reduced, as was the import of tobacco and petrol. Britain had been living on an American loan, and the loan had leaked away more quickly than anyone had thought possible. In August, when the populace was dining on soya beans and Egyptian eggs, the Prime Minister announced a new plan for austerity, and with a shudder people heard that the American film-producers had decided to stop sending motion-pictures to Britain. There were more food-cuts, and more dry petrol-pumps; and the Home Secretary appealed for a national effort to stop the rot.

In Edinburgh the response was immediate. By the end of the month the pervading darkness had been torn apart by brilliant remonstrance, and a vision that had appeared to three remarkable men was realised. The men were Harry Harvey Wood, a senior official of the British Council; Rudolf Bing, who later become Director of the Metropolitan Opera House in New York; and Sir John Falconer, Lord Provost of the City – and their vision was an International Festival of Music and Drama. In all its history Edinburgh had had no experience of such an undertaking, and the gloom that had rewarded our astonishing victory in a long and unnecessary war was aggravated by local scepticism about the native ability to house so vast and glittering an enterprise. But the faith of Falconer, Bing and Harvey Wood persisted against immediate doubt and general apathy, and into Edinburgh came the Glyndebourne Opera Company to present *The Marriage of Figaro* and Verdi's *Macbeth*; the Vienna State Orchestra under Bruno Walter to let Beethoven speak for glory; Louis Jouvet from Paris to bring Giraudoux and Molière into the alliance; and also from France l'Orchestre des Concerts Colonne under Paul Paray. The Hallé and the Scottish Orchestras arrived; the Old Vic and the Sadler's Wells Ballet; Kathleen Ferrier to sing Mahler's *Das Lied von der Erde*, and Schnabel, Szigeti, Primrose and Fournier to play chamber music by Schubert and Brahms.

Triumph was the consequence of their advent; and darkness shivered and retreated. It was a triumph of courage, of faith in a vision; a triumph of elegance over drab submission to the penalties of emerging victorious from a modern war. The music critic of the *Scotsman* was so moved as to write, in his review of a concert by the French orchestra: 'Let us salute Paul Paray and his players, and in saluting them take up afresh the battle against all slovenly and spiritless things.'

That, clearly enunciated, was a battle-cry for elegance which, if it had been heard and followed, would have saved us the spleen of much modern writing, painting and dramatic experiment. It was too demanding a battle-cry, but a natural response to M. Paray who, when he conducted his orchestra in the British national anthem, that so often sounds as if it were a lamentation for the pains of authority, made it clamour like a reveille bidding all good men to wake and bare their swords for a crusading monarch – and in the flash and inspiration of the fiddle-bows, imagined blades reflected the sunshine. Week after week the real, the visible sun, poured down its light on the town, and elegance in a hundred ways informed its life.

Bibliography

Antiquarian Repertory, The, Volume IV, London, 1809

ARNOT, HUGO, *The History of Edinburgh*, Edinburgh, 1799

BOSWELL, JAMES, *Journal of a Tour to the Hebrides with Samuel Johnson LL.D.*, London, 1785.

BRERETON, SIR WILLIAM, *Diary of Sir William Brereton*, London, 1844.

BRITTON, JOHN, *Modern Athens, Displayed in a Series of Views of Edinburgh in the Nineteenth Century, from Original Drawings by Mr Thomas H. Shepherd*, London, 1829.

BROME, JAMES, Travels over England, Scotland and Wales, London, 1700.

BURT, EDWARD, *Letters from a Gentleman in the North of Scotland to his Friend in England*, London, 1754.

CALDERWOOD, DAVID, *The History of the Kirk of Scotland*, edited by Thomas Thomson, Edinburgh, 1842.

CARLYLE, DR ALEXANDER, OF INVERESK, *Autobiography 1722–1805*, edited by J. Hill Burton, London, 1860.

CARLYLE, THOMAS, *Reminiscences*, London, 1887.

COCKBURN, LORD HENRY, *Memorials of His Time*, Edinburgh, 1856.

— *The Journal of Henry Cockburn, 1831–1854*, Edinburgh, 1874.

— *Life of Lord Jeffrey*, Edinburgh, 1852.

COLSTON, JAMES, *The Town and Port of Leith*, Edinburgh, 1892.

DAICHES, DAVID, *Was: A Pastime from Time Past*, London, 1975.

— *Two Worlds*, London, 1956.

DEFOE, DANIEL, *The Letters of Daniel Defoe*, edited by G.H. Healey, Oxford, 1955.

— *Tour thro' the Whole Island of Britain*, London, 1726.

Description of Scotland, written at first by Hector Boethius in Latin and afterwards translated into the Scottish Speech by John Bellenden, Archdeacon of Murray, and now finallie in English by W. H., Arbroath, 1805.

FLETCHER, MRS ELIZA, *Autobiography 1770–1858*, Edinburgh, 1875.

FORSYTH, ROBERT, *The Beauties of Scotland*, Edinburgh, 1805.

GILBERT, W.M., (ed.) *Edinburgh in the Nineteenth Century, being a diary of the chief events which have occurred in the city from 1800 AD to 1900 AD*, Edinburgh, 1901.

GRANT OF ROTHIEMURCHUS, ELIZABETH, *Memoirs of a Highland Lady 1797–1827*, revised and edited by Angus Davidson, London, 1950.

GRANT, JAMES, *Old and New Edinburgh*, London, 1883.

GRANT OF LAGGAN, MRS, *Memoirs and Correspondence*, London, 1844.

HERON, ROBERT, *Scotland Delineated*, Edinburgh, 1799.

HOME, JOHN, *The History of the Rebellion in the Year 1745*, London, 1802.

HOWELL, JAMES, *Epistolae Ho-Elianae: Familiar Letters Domestic and Forren*, London, 1655.

HUME OF GODSCROFT, DAVID, *A General History of Scotland, Together with a Particular History of the Houses of Douglas and Angus*, Edinburgh, 1644.

Kay's Edinburgh Portraits, Written by James Paterson and Edited by James Maidment, London, 1885.

KIRKTON, JAMES, *The Secret and True History of the Church of Scotland from the Restoration to the year 1678*, Edinburgh, 1817.

KNOX, JOHN, *The History of the Reformation in Scotland*, edited by C.J. Guthrie, London, 1898.

LAUDER OF FOUNTAINHALL, SIR JOHN, *Chronological Notes of Scottish Affairs from 1680 till 1701*, Edinburgh, 1822.

LINDSAY, ROBERT, OF PITTSCOTTIE, *The History of Scotland from 1436 to 1565*, Glasgow, 1749.

LINKLATER, ERIC, *Edinburgh*, London, 1960.

LOCKHART OF CARNWATH, GEORGE, *Memoirs Concerning the Affairs of Scotland*, London, 1714.

LOCKHART, J.G., *Peter's Letters to his Kinsfolk*, Edinburgh, 1819.

—*The Life of Sir Walter Scott*, Edinburgh, 1832.

MACKENZIE, HENRY, *Anecdotes and Egotisms*, edited by H. W. Thompson, London, 1927.

MASSON, DAVID, *Memoirs of Two Cities*, Edinburgh and Aberdeen, 1911.

Minutes of the proceedings in parliament, Edinburgh, 1707.

MORYSON, FYNES, *An Itinerary Written by Fynes Moryson, gent.*, London, 1617.

MUIR, EDWIN, *Scottish Journey*, London, 1935.

NAPIER, MARK, *Memoirs of the Marquis of Montrose*, Edinburgh, 1856.

NICOLL, JOHN, *A Diary of Public Transactions and Other Occurrences Chiefly in Scotland from 1650 to 1667*, Edinburgh, 1836.

PENNANT, THOMAS, *A Tour in Scotland MDCCLXIX*, London, 1774.

Proposals for Carrying on Certain Public Works in the City of Edinburgh, Edinburgh, 1752.

ROTHES, JOHN, EARL OF, *A Relation of the Proceedings concerning the Affairs of the Kirk of Scotland*, Edinburgh, 1830.

RUTHEN, LORD, *A Relation of the Death of David Rizzio, chief favorite to Mary Stuart Queen of Scotland*, London, 1699.

SCOTT, WALTER, *Tales of a Grandfather*, Edinburgh, 1829.

—*The Heart of Midlothian*, Edinburgh, 1818.

—*The Prose works of Sir Walter Scott*, Edinburgh, 1834.

—General Preface to Author's Edition of the Waverley Novels, Edinburgh, 1819

SMELLIE, WILLIAM, *Literary and Characteristical Lives of Gregory, Kames, Hume and Smith*, Edinburgh, 1800.

SMOLLET, TOBIAS, *Humphry Clinker*, London, 1771.

SPALDING, JOHN, *History of the Troubles and Memorable Transactions in Scotland and England from M.DC.XXIV to M.DL.XLV*, Edinburgh, 1828.

STEVENSON, ROBERT LOUIS, *Edinburgh, Picturesque Notes*, London, 1879.

TAYLOR, JOHN, *The Pennyles Pilgrimage: or the money-less perambulation of John Taylor from London to Edenborough*, London, 1618.

TOPHAM, CAPTAIN EDWARD, *Letters from Edinburgh; Written in the Years 1774 and 1775*, London, 1776.

Weekly Magazine, or Edinburgh Amusement, the, Edinburgh, 1773.

WILSON, SIR DANIEL, *Memorials of Edinburgh in the Olden Time*, Edinburgh, 1891.

WODROW, REVD ROBERT, *The History of the Sufferings of the Church of Scotland*, Volume IV, Glasgow, 1830.

WORDSWORTH, DOROTHY, *Recollection of a Tour Made in Scotland AD 1803*, Edinburgh, 1874.

Index

Numbers in *italics* refer to illustrations

GENERAL INDEX

Date Due